S0-AEB-493

Kilimanjaro

Summit of Africa

Jacquetta Megarry

Kilimanjaro: Summit of Africa

First published in 2009 by Rucksack Readers, Landrick Lodge, Dunblane, FK15 0HY, UK
+44/0 1786 824 696 web: **www.rucsacs.com** email: info@rucsacs.com

ISBN: 978-1-898481-52-2

Designed in Scotland by WorkHorse **www.workhorse.co.uk**

Colour separation by HK Scanner Arts International Ltd in Hong Kong; printed in China by
Hong Kong Graphics & Printing Ltd

Feedback request
The publisher welcomes comments and updates from readers on any aspect of this book:
please email us at **info@rucsacs.com**.

Disclaimer
A trip to climb Mount Kilimanjaro may involve risks of personal injury, ill-health
and even, if good advice is ignored, death. Readers, even if in excellent general
health, should consult their medical advisers before committing to an expedition
to extreme altitude. This book offers information and advice on minimising
and managing the dangers. However, you are responsible for your own safety.
**Neither author nor publisher can accept any liability for any ill-health or
accident arising directly or indirectly from reading this book**.

Facts were checked carefully prior to publication, but things can change at any
time. Please check our Kilimanjaro page links and forum for updates:
www.rucsacs.com/books/Kilimanjaro and **www.rucsacs.com/forum**

Contents

The seven summits

Denali

This book is for anybody who wants to climb Kili, whether as their first venture to extreme altitude, or as the first tick on their list of the 'seven summits'.

Of the seven continental summits, five are clear and two controversial: see the table on p5. Whilst the summits of Africa, North and South America, Antarctica and Asia are undisputed, debate persists about Australasia and Europe. The problem is that there is no watertight definition of a continent: see www.7summits.com.

Dick Bass was the first to complete and popularise the idea of a seven summits list (with Kosciuszko). By late 2008 the number of completers was 234 Nearly all regarded Elbrus, in the Caucasus, as their European summit, although most would also have climbed Mont Blanc anyway: see www.7summits.com/stats.

Equator

Aconcagua

Vinson

Overall difficulty grading

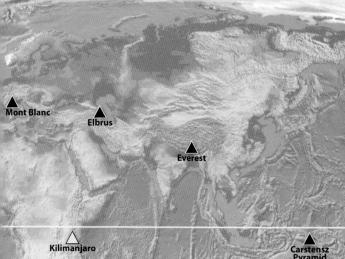

Kosciuszko		Elbrus	Aconcagua		Everest	9000
	Kilimanjaro			Denali		8000
		Mont Blanc	Carstensz	Vinson		7000
			Pyramid			6000
1	**2**	**3**	**4**	**5**	**6** **7** **8** **9**

Mont Blanc

Elbrus

Everest

Kilimanjaro

Carstensz Pyramid

Kosciuszko

Summary of altitudes and technical difficulty

Continent	Summit	Country	Altitude (metres)	Altitude (feet)	Technical difficulty
Africa	**Kilimanjaro**	**Tanzania**	**5895**	**19340**	**2**
Antarctica	Vinson	Antarctica	4897	16065	4-5
Asia	Everest	Nepal/China	8848	29029	7
Australasia	Carstensz Pyramid	Papua, Irian Jaya	4884	16025	8-9
Australia	Kosciuszko	Australia	2228	7310	1
Europe	Elbrus	Russia	5642	18510	4
Europe, western	Mont Blanc	France	4810	15780	4
North America	Denali (McKinley)	USA	6194	20320	5
South America	Aconcagua	Argentina	6962	22840	3

With a summit at nearly 6000m, Kilimanjaro is the highest free-standing mountain in the world. Rising majestically several miles above the East African plains, the massif makes an outstanding landmark, its very name *Uhuru* a powerful symbol of freedom. People are lured from all over the word by the romantic notion that ordinary people with no technical experience can reach the 'roof of Africa'. It's merely a hike – albeit a strenuous one.

The natural world on this mountain is extraordinary. In a landscape formed by ice and fire, the ascent takes you from tropical rain forest to arctic conditions among the summit glaciers. The variety of life forms, and their adaptation to extreme condtions, is fascinating. At sea level, such contrasts would be 10,000 km apart. On Kilimanjaro, you walk from equator to pole in a few days.

Everyone who attempts Kili will reach deeply inside themselves. Most people describe summit day as the hardest physical task they have ever tried. Attaining the summit is not the only goal, however: success lies rather in the quality of the attempt and what you learn from other members of your team.

For me, Kili brought self-belief that led to the foundation of a new business and lifestyle. Between 1999 and 2008 I made four journeys to Uhuru, each by a different route. Each was an unforgettable landmark in my personal and professional life.

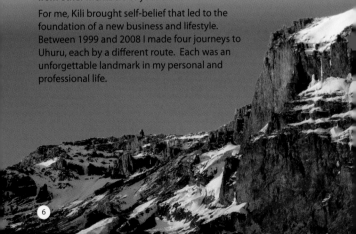

'Strange as it may sound, Kilimanjaro is perhaps one of the most dangerous mountains in the world' (UIAA Medical Commission, 2009). Seemingly accessible to anyone who can sustain a strenuous hike for several days, Kili is a trap for the unwary. The human body cannot acclimatise to extreme altitude inside a week, and individuals vary widely in their ability to cope.

No amount of preparation can guarantee success. Two approaches to the altitude problem can greatly improve your chances, however:
a) acclimatise on another mountain *immediately* before tackling Kili
b) choose a route and itinerary with extra nights at high altitude.

We recommend that you climb Mount Meru first, if possible. Its location, altitude and profile make it ideal. Mount Kenya is another option, but Meru is by far the closest mountain of suitable height and it's an exhilarating volcanic hike in its own right: see pp52-61.

Various Kili route options are discussed on pp15-20 and tabulated on p17. Decide your preference *before* choosing your tour operator, because some offer only a restricted choice of routes. Read the descriptions in Part 4 and consider any variations before committing. Some, such as overnighting in Karanga, require an extra day and must be booked ahead. Others, such as using Kosovo rather than Barafu, may be possible by agreement with your guide on the mountain, especially within a small group: see p69.

The air fare to Tanzania will be a major part of your holiday cost, so consider spending more time in this wonderful country. Take a wildlife safari, go to the spice islands of Zanzibar and Pemba, or visit the Great Rift Valley and Olduvai Gorge.

To visit the famous 'northern circuit' National Parks (Serengeti, Tarangire and Ngorongoro) you really need an extra week, as for Amboseli and Tsavo which are across the border in Kenya. The massive Selous Game Reserve is much further away to the south, and combines well with flying back from Dar es Salaam.

Even if you can spare only one extra day, don't miss the chance of a game drive in Arusha National Park. It has a wide range of animals, including baboon, wild buffalo, colobus monkey and hippopotamus, and it's famous for its giraffes (Tanzania's national animal). Bird life is spectacular, ranging from flamingos, secretary birds and eagles to colourful sunbirds and bee-eaters.

What is the best time of year?

Because Kilimanjaro is so near the equator (3° S), the midday sun is always nearly overhead and the seasons are not like those at higher latitude. Two rainy seasons bring poor visibility and slippery paths, and run from late March to mid-June and November to December. Avoid them if possible, especially if you hope to climb Mount Meru. Generally, January to early March and late June to mid-October are the best times to go. But mountains make their own weather, and heavy rain or snow, high winds and thunderstorms can affect Kili at any time: see photograph below.

Expect a huge daily temperature range – up to 20-30°C by day on the lower slopes, and down to -15 or -20°C or lower at night. At any altitude, expect to feel very cold at night. Higher up, daytime temperatures are lower, and winds tend to be stronger, but rain and snow are less likely. Be aware of the chill factor and prepare for it.

Kibo Camp in the 'dry' season (2004)

8

You will certainly feel very cold at the night-time start of your summit climb, but may warm up once you get going. At any time of year, at any altitude, you need clothing that works well in layers, good waterproofs and a roomy backpack to carry excess clothing.

Think also about the moon's phases. You can plan for a full moon to light your night-time summit attempt: see p97 for a website link.

Insurance

Standard holiday insurance may not suffice for Kili. Some policies have exclusions and altitude limits. Read the small print and if in doubt ask the insurers. Annual worldwide policies may provide adequate cover, or may be upgraded at low cost. Mountaineering clubs and councils often offer very good rates on separate policies.

The time to take out insurance is when you first commit yourself to expenditure – to the expedition and/or the flight, whichever is the sooner. That way, if you are unlucky enough to have a training accident or family emergency, you will be covered for cancellation or postponement costs. Although helicopter rescue is not an option, evacuation and medical costs can be very steep.

Rescue vehicle for emergencies

1 Planning and preparation
1·2 Choosing your tour operator

It's vital to choose your tour operator wisely. In most countries, any company that sells Kili trips work with one of a few reliable ground operators in Tanzania. Most are based in Moshi and a few in Arusha. Their prices obviously reflect their profit margin and local company share, as well as the costs of staffing offices, marketing and brochures. However, it's worth researching the prices before booking. In June 2008 we met a group of Americans who had paid $3800 for a Lemosho itinerary nearly identical to that we had bought for $1700. They had the same Tanzanian local outfitter, with the same level of food, equipment and porter support.

At the other extreme, you could ask around in Moshi or make direct contact by email and find much lower prices. Beware of the dubious operators that sell unfeasibly short trips at prices that are far too low. For the clients, these itineraries are likely to end in failure to summit, ill-health or even danger. For the guides and porters, they invariably mean unacceptably poor treatment (excessive loads to carry, inadequate food and clothing and exploitative low wages). A 'bargain basement' trip may turn out to exclude Park fees, to use vehicles that break down with staff who demand dollars urgently for fuel. There are many reasons why brochure prices in developed countries seem high compared with prices available locally.

Better value than either, if you are happy to organise your own flights, is to book through **www.7summits.com** – an outfit run by Harry Kikstra, author of three other books in this series: see back cover. He works with a reliable Moshi company and because his system is web-based the prices are much lower than you would pay through a conventional tour company. Personally I have been up Kili four times, twice using a British holiday company that worked with Shah Tours, Moshi and latterly twice via 7summits.com whose partner was Zara Tours, Moshi. All four trips were well organised and resourced, with staff who were well treated and helpful.

One reason that all Kili trips seem expensive is that the Tanzanian National Park Authority (TANAPA) charges each hiker a hefty daily fee. Sadly, this system encourages people to attempt the mountain too quickly, resulting in avoidable altitude sickness. And because wages in Tanzania are so low, the Park fees make up a high proportion of the total costs of the land-based part of your trip. For most hikers, the trip to Tanzania is a large commitment in time and air fares, so it's worth spending an extra day or two to make the climb healthy and enjoyable.

When choosing a tour operator, look for the following:
- a good choice of routes with enough nights at high altitude to acclimatise
- flexible departure dates to suit your needs: starting your hike mid-week can help to avoid crowded trails, and you may wish to combine Kili with other visits
- a responsible approach to porter welfare and the environment
- clarity about what is included in the price (Park fees, camping gear, hotel nights)
- food, tents and equipment of adequate quality
- if flights are included, aim to fly direct to Kilimanjaro International Airport. (From Nairobi you face a long overland shuttle with Kenyan border delays, or an extra connecting flight, although prices tend to be lower.)

Before finalising your dates, consider the advantages of a rest day on arrival, especially if you have a long flight and expect to suffer from jet lag. You may welcome a spare day to overcome dehydration from the flight, to allow lost baggage to arrive and to adjust to the change of food and water.

Before committing yourself to a departure date, decide how much preparation time you need, not only for physical training, but also for other tasks: see the checklist on p29.

Planning and preparation
1·3 Porters, guides and trekkers

Readers accustomed to being self-reliant on a mountain will experience culture shock on Kili. If you expected to carry your own kit and make your own camps and meals, you may feel uneasy when you discover that the support team does it all. Porters carry baggage, tents and supplies for the whole group. They set up and break down camp, and they also prepare, serve and wash up after meals. A team may even set up a special tent with portable toilet, later emptying it into the campsite long-drop toilets, then carry it to the next camp.

The porters move with amazing speed over rough, steep terrain, carrying huge loads on their heads, often with hands in pockets, hardly ever falling. They move much faster than trekkers, overtaking them on their way to set up the next camp. The guide deals with route-finding, usually placing an assistant guide or porter as backstop. Trekkers are expected to walk at their own pace anywhere between the two.

You have little alternative to being looked after. For a start, you won't be allowed through the Park gates without a licensed guide. Although hiring porters is in theory optional, in practice Tanzanians almost invariably carry loads for tourists. You'll see lots of porters hanging around the Park gates, competing for work that each of them badly needs.

Especially on a first visit to Africa, many Westerners feel uncomfortable about the idea of using a guide and relying on 'native porters'. You may also be amazed by the sheer number of people in the support team – typically, at least two porters per hiker, plus a cook (perhaps with an assistant) and at least one guide.

Porters' loads vary with the route: up to 15kg (Machame/Lemosho) or up to 18kg (Marangu/Rongai), excluding their personal kit. This is a heavy load compared with the trekker's, whose rucksack may weigh only 4-8kg. At one level, this is obviously unfair.

On the other hand, the trekkers' holidays pay the porters' wages, and the tips are vital to them and their families. Porters' pay is very poor by Western standards, but still is far above the Tanzanian norm.

After three years' experience, porters may progress to become assistant guides, and a year or two later may reach the rank of head guide. Guides are better paid than porters, normally carry only their own equipment, have some training and speak some English.

Guides and porters are very fit, agile and are mostly well-acclimatised to altitude. But they are human, they also feel tired and sometimes they too suffer altitude symptoms. Porters may be too frightened of losing their jobs to admit to symptoms, even if they recognise the cause. They also suffer from the cold because of poor equipment. Tragically, there have been several porter deaths from hypothermia and AMS – avoidable with warmer clothing and greater awareness. You can help by stopping and expressing concern for a porter who looks cold or ill, and by asking your tour operator (preferably before booking with them) what steps they take to ensure fair pay and conditions for porters: see p97.

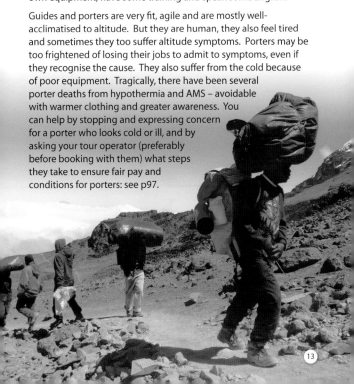

Guides tend to be better equipped than porters, but because they have to walk at the slow pace of the visitors, they may feel colder. Grateful tourists sometimes donate the odd item of clothing or gear at the end of the trip, and the guide may operate a system for sharing such extras. This is no substitute for fair wages and adequate tips (see panel below).

In the Tanzanian context, tipping is not optional, it's a legitimate expectation. Withhold or reduce tips only in the very unlikely case of poor service, and explain clearly what was wrong. Most of the staff are very hard-working and polite, and they appreciate a short ceremony for handing over the tips. Large groups may prefer to hand over the whole kitty to the head guide for distribution, but it's more personal to tip and thank porters individually. Be prepared to tip on the last trekking day, because the team sometimes disperses as soon as it reaches the Park gates.

Wages and tips: how much?

Different operators pay different rates to their staff, and fierce competition keeps the overall level low. On average, in 2009 the daily wage was (US dollar equivalent) about $4-8 per porter, $5-9 for the cook, $6-10 for Assistant Guides and $10-15 for the Head Guide. However budget operators pay less than this, some much less. If you have paid too little for your Kili package, you may have colluded in this exploitation: try to make amends through generous tipping. With Park fees of $400-$800 per person, be suspicious of tours that don't cost enough. Where margins are tight, the porters' wages will be the first to suffer.

Tour operators normally offer guidance about tipping. If wages are unusually high, lesser tipping might be in order. If service was extra special, be more generous. The amount also depends somewhat on the group size and route. As a general guideline you should allow about 10% of the cost of your tour (excluding air fare) for the whole team, dividing the kitty roughly in proportion to wage rates given above.

1 Planning and preparation
1·4 Choosing your route

The number of route names and permutations can be confusing at first. This book focuses on the four most popular trekking routes: Machame, Lemosho, Marangu and Rongai, and explains some other options on pp19-20. For a quick overview, see the route profiles and Table 1 on pp16-17. The map (inside back cover) shows these four and some variations. They fall naturally into two pairs: the Lemosho ascent joins the Machame route on the Shira Plateau, after which they are identical, and the Rongai approach joins Marangu at Kibo Hut, after which they too are identical.

Marangu, the original and still one of the most popular routes, is named after the village to the east of the massif. It's the only one where you sleep overnight in bunk-bedded huts with solar-powered electricity, and there are toilet blocks nearby with running water. Marangu is also known as the 'tourist' or 'Coca-Cola' route, because soft drinks and water are on sale. Most huts sleep up to six, except Kibo Hut which has 60 bunks in five dormitories. People of either sex are allocated to bunks on arrival, so don't expect privacy. But sleeping in a hut is warmer than camping.

Marangu is also the cheapest option, and although busy, at least the number of bunks limits overall numbers. Avoid itineraries that offer Marangu as a 3-day ascent. Unless already acclimatised, you need *at least* one extra night, taken at Horombo. This isn't high enough for good acclimatisation, but it's the only option. Marangu is the only route on which you go back the same way as you came.

If you prefer variety and enjoy camping, choose Rongai, Machame or Lemosho. You sleep normally two to a tent, using a headtorch for lighting. The latrines (toilets) are generally more primitive and further away, although your team may have a private toilet tent. Rongai approaches from the north and descends south-east via Marangu, camping near the huts. Rongai also offers direct and indirect alternatives: see p89.

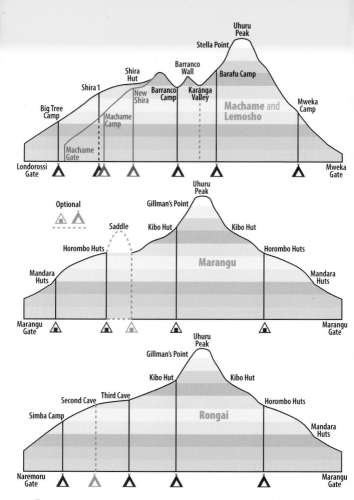

Machame and **Lemosho**

Uhuru Peak
Stella Point
Barranco Wall
Barafu Camp
Shira Hut
Shira 1
New Shira
Barranco Camp
Karanga Valley
Mweka Camp
Big Tree Camp
Machame Camp
Machame Gate
Londorossi Gate
Mweka Gate

Marangu

Optional
Saddle
Uhuru Peak
Gillman's Point
Kibo Hut
Kibo Hut
Horombo Huts
Horombo Huts
Mandara Huts
Mandara Huts
Marangu Gate
Marangu Gate

Rongai

Uhuru Peak
Gillman's Point
Kibo Hut
Kibo Hut
Second Cave
Third Cave
Simba Camp
Horombo Huts
Mandara Huts
Naremoru Gate
Marangu Gate

On Machame, you ascend from the south via Machame Gate. After ascending via Barafu, you descend by the more direct Mweka route. Lemosho involves a long approach from the west, and because it's much less busy, you'll see signs of large animals – buffalo, elephant or even lion. These are more strenuous routes than the other two, because

• you walk further, with more ascent and descent
• the terrain is tougher so the hiking takes more effort.

To summarise, if you wish to avoid camping, or if budget is the main factor, choose Marangu. Otherwise, choose Rongai, which is both easier and more flexible than Marangu, has more variety and fewer people, albeit a longer journey before beginning your hike. If you relish the challenge of some easy scrambling and are confident of your fitness, choose the more scenic Machame route, or, if you can spare an extra day and a bit more expense, upgrade to Lemosho. If you find the choice difficult, read Part 4 carefully and visit our website forum: **www.rucsacs.com/forum**. There are lots of diary accounts of every route on the web.

Table 1: Summary of Kilimanjaro's main routes

Route	Book sections	Days for ascent	Overnight	Grade*	Comments
Machame	4.1	4 or 5	camping	B/C	scenic route; involves some easy scrambling
Lemosho	4.2	5 or 6	camping	B/C	approaches from west, then links to Machame ascent
Marangu	4.3	4	huts	B	3-day ascent possible if acclimatised
Rongai	4.4	4	camping	B	direct route (if pre-acclimatised)
		5		A / B	direct or indirect
		6		A	indirect route
Descent (all routes)	*4.5*	*+2*			*first 'descent' day includes the overnight summit attempt*
Overall total		6 to 8			the longer your trip, the greater your chance of summiting enjoyably

* A means easy, C is moderate, E is very strenuous; route grading excludes summit day which is D/E in all cases.

How does route choice affect your chances of summiting? Overall, 'success' rates for Marangu hover around the 50% level, although some operators claim 70% or more. The average is depressed by low-budget, minimum-stay tourists who omit the extra night at Horombo, a false economy because most people suffer altitude sickness as a result.

Higher percentages are quoted for Machame, Lemosho and Rongai, but this doesn't mean you improve your personal chances by avoiding Marangu. Fit, experienced hikers are attracted to the other routes, and they are more likely to succeed than the budget tourist on Marangu. Exertion is a major risk factor in altitude sickness. If your main aim is to maximise your chance of reaching the summit, choose Rongai or Marangu, which have only one seriously taxing day. On a 6-day Machame, your summit attempt comes after four fairly strenuous days of trekking, and is immediately followed by a prolonged descent.

Reaching the summit, however, is not everything. There are good reasons why many people prefer longer and more scenic routes. Machame can be made less strenuous if your itinerary adds an overnight in Karanga Valley. The Lemosho route is a 7- or 8-day itinerary and gives you a much better chance to acclimatise. It also has fewer hikers and more wildlife sightings.

Overall, Marangu is the cheapest route, with Rongai next, then Machame, and Lemosho the most expensive. This mainly reflects the time spent on the mountain, because Park fees and wages are charged by the day. Any route becomes more expensive, and also more likely to succeed, if you include extra days at high altitude. The longer your trek, the greater your chances of summiting enjoyably. And once you take in the cost of your flight to Tanzania, saving two hundred dollars or so may seem less important than choosing the best possible itinerary.

Other options

You may hear about some further route choices, such as Shira and Umbwe. Shira is a seldom-used variant of Lemosho: you are driven straight to the Morum Barrier Gate at 3400m, and begin your hike above the forest zone on the Shira Plateau, with little opportunity to acclimatise. Unless you add extra nights to this short route, it is suitable only for those who have already acclimatised. Umbwe is a steep trail that takes you direct to Barranco via Umbwe Cave, less busy than most, and little used because of its steep, treacherous terrain, and because almost everybody would then need an extra night at Barranco. However, Umbwe offers some spectacular views, and it's the route where the IMAX movie was filmed.

The Western Breach is a huge gap in the crater rim that creates a short-cut to the crater via the ruins of Arrow Glacier Hut. The climb involves steep, icy scree and rock, sometimes requiring technical equipment, and used to be offered widely as a more challenging finale to the Machame/Umbwe ascents.

Scrambling up the Barranco Wall

However, the route was closed after a fatal rockfall in January 2006. About 40 tonnes of rock loosened by melting ice-scree slid steeply downhill at speeds of 40 kph (25 mph), killing three tourists, an unknown number of Tanzanians and seriously injuring many more. Although it reopened in December 2007, some experts consider it unduly dangerous, and many responsible operators no longer offer it, whilst others require a special indemnity form. If considering this option, refer to **www.westernbreach.co.uk** – especially to its videos and the report of the accident investigation.

A final variation is the option of making camp in the crater, which is expensive (several hundred dollars per person) because of the extra work to move the whole team and gear to such high altitude. Normally porters and their loads go no higher than Barafu (4600m). Crater Camp (5790m) demands much more effort from the whole team, and in extreme weather it sometimes has to be rearranged.

To sleep at extreme altitude, you need to be better acclimatised than to make a brief visit to the summit. Staying in the crater is feasible only as an agreed part of one of the longer itineraries, and even then it's offered only by some companies, subject to conditions. When all goes well, you make the 5-6-hour ascent from Barafu in daylight, and stay at Crater Camp, perhaps also visiting the Reusch Crater with its Ash Pit. Next day, the summit climb takes only a couple of hours, avoiding the midnight start of other itineraries.

Crater Camp, near the Furtwangler Glacier

The altitude problem is the shortage of oxygen: as you climb higher, the air gets thinner. At 5500m (18,000ft), atmospheric pressure is 50% of that at sea level, and at the summit of Kili (5895m) lower still. You might expect that breathing twice as fast as at sea level would let you take in as much oxygen. Sadly, the reality is much worse. The lungs' ability to extract oxygen deteriorates rapidly with altitude, much faster than the decline in oxygen pressure. Furthermore, when climbing at altitude on difficult terrain, your muscles need more oxygen anyway.

Red blood cells (greatly magnified)

Your heart is the pump that makes your blood circulate. The lungs load oxygen into your red blood cells for delivery to your muscles and other vital organs. The oxygen demand from your muscles depends on their activity level, but your brain also needs its share. Despite having only 2% of your body weight, your brain needs 15% of its oxygen. If it gets less, judgement declines, control suffers and speech may become confused.

Your body responds in various ways to needing more oxygen:

- you breathe faster and deeper
- your heart beats faster, increasing the oxygen reaching your tissues and forcing blood into parts of your lungs that aren't normally used
- your body expels excess fluid and creates more red blood cells, making the blood thicker.

These changes happen over different time-scales. You start to breathe faster right away. Your heart rate rises within minutes. After several days, your blood starts to thicken. If you find yourself urinating a lot that is a probably a sign that your body is acclimatising well. Creating more red blood cells takes longer still, at least a week, and is irrelevant to most Kili itineraries.

You can help yourself to acclimatise by breathing deeply, and by drinking plenty of water. Sleep is an important time for the body's adjustment: avoid sleeping pills and alcohol, which depress breathing. Standard trekking advice is to limit daily altitude gain to 300m, but the spacing of campsites on Kili makes that impossible, so acclimatisation should be a major factor in deciding your itinerary.

Acute Mountain Sickness (AMS)

Acute Mountain Sickness is the medical term for altitude or mountain sickness, but 'acute' only means 'sudden-onset'. AMS symptoms, if mild or moderate, often disappear if the victim rests or ascends no further. If AMS is severe, the victim must descend.

No expert nor textbook can predict whether or how you will be affected. If you can't face the possibility that you might 'fail' due to AMS, then don't attempt it. Gender is a factor: females are less likely to experience AMS than males. At moderate altitude, young people are more likely to

Complications from AMS (HAPE & HACE)

Edema (or oedema) simply means swelling. HAPE and HACE are High Altitude Pulmonary Edema and High Altitude Cerebral Edema. They are serious complications, caused by swelling of tissues in the lungs and brain respectively. HAPE can occur anywhere above 2500m (8200ft) and HACE above 3000m (9850ft). The risks therefore exist at any time from your first night onward, albeit more probably at higher altitudes, and amongst those who ascend quickly.

HAPE is caused by fluid from tiny blood vessels leaking into the lungs. It affects perhaps 2% of those at altitude, usually people who already have some AMS symptoms. Cold, exercise and dehydration all increase the risk of HAPE. So does gender: males are 5-6 times more likely to be affected than females, and children are more at risk than adults. About 10% of HAPE victims will die unless promptly diagnosed and treated.

The HAPE sufferer typically looks and feels ill, and

- has serious difficulty in breathing, which may be noisy or 'crackly'
- is very weak and cannot sustain exercise
- has a rapid pulse and perhaps a fever
- may have blue-looking lips, ears and fingernail-beds
- has a cough; if there is pink or frothy sputum, the case is serious.

In HACE, swollen blood vessels in the brain cause pressure to build up, causing some or all of: ataxia, dizziness, extreme fatigue, vomiting, acute headache, disorientation, hallucinations, loss of vision, numbness or personality change. Unless treated promptly – by immediate descent, oxygen and suitable drugs – HACE leads to coma and death.

suffer than their elders: the risk decreases in an almost straight line with age. Individuals vary widely, and even at a given altitude, the same person may be fine one time, yet severely ill when they return.

You need to be fit to climb Kili, but your fitness will not *of itself* reduce your chances of suffering AMS. Over-exertion is a risk factor in AMS, and at a given ascent rate, greater fitness reduces oxygen demand. In practice, however, ultra-fit individuals are more likely to try to ascend too quickly, thus making themselves more vulnerable.

Degrees of AMS

The distinctions between mild, moderate and severe AMS are not watertight, but a useful shortcut is provided by the points system: see Table 2.

Severe AMS can be life-threatening. The victim's judgement is affected and the complications (HAPE and HACE) can be lethal: see the panel on p22. If you follow good advice, you are very unlikely to experience these, but should know about them – it might help you recognise another person's problems.

Table 2:	AMS points	Interpretation		
symptom	**points**	**total**	**degree of AMS**	**treatment**
headache	1	1-3	*mild*	drink fluids, pain-killer, rest
insomnia	1			
nausea or loss of appetite	1			
dizziness	1	4-6	*moderate*	drink fluids, pain-killer, no more ascent until better
headache (resistant to pain-killers)	2			
vomiting	2			
breathing difficulty at rest	3			
abnormal fatigue	3	7+	*severe*	emergency medication and immediate descent
low urine production	3			
wet noise when breathing	7			
loss of vision	7			

It's ideal if you have a friend along with you, so you can monitor each other's behaviour. Severe AMS is avoidable and treatable, as long as people are aware of its symptoms and take it seriously.

Mild AMS is common on Kili, but anyone with symptoms should be monitored closely in case they worsen. Assess the sufferer's condition first thing in the morning: symptoms that persist after resting should be taken very seriously. See the panel for information about Diamox. Many climbers believe that it should be reserved for use as treatment, not prevention. Others prefer herbal alternatives such as ginkgo biloba: there is evidence that this reduces symptoms if started 3-5 days before climbing.

Finger probe measuring blood oxygen

AMS Summary

To reduce the risk of AMS:

- choose an itinerary with extra nights at altitude
- ascend slowly
- drink lots of water
- keep warm, eat regularly and look after yourself.

Be alert for AMS:

- monitor your own and your fellow climbers' acclimatisation
- apply the points system to any symptoms: see Table 2, p23

If AMS strikes:

- if it is mild, drink more water, rest and take a pain-killer
- if symptoms persist or are more serious, do the above and do not ascend further
- if symptoms are severe or with complications, **descend immediately** and seek medical help.

The treatment of altitude-related illness is to stop further ascent and, if symptoms are severe or getting worse, to descend. Oxygen, drugs and other treatments for altitude illness should be viewed as adjuncts to aid descent.
British Medical Journal vol 326, 26.4.2003

Individual reactions

From a hiker whose behaviour became erratic at altitude on the Machame route.

" *The disorientation crept up on me and I wasn't in any state of mind to diagnose what was going on ... If your mind isn't functioning fully, how will you know that your mind isn't functioning fully?* "

The author's experience

" *On my first ascent (Marangu, 1999) I had no AMS symptoms, although 7 out of 16 in our group were too unwell to summit. The next year, on a 6-day Machame, I had moderate AMS after the third day. I recovered overnight to reach the summit (2000m higher) symptom-free, 24 hours later. Others in our group first suffered AMS only when approaching the crater rim, several so badly that they had to turn back.*

On a third trip (Rongai, 2004) I was symptom-free, I believe because of having summited Mt Meru just before. Finally, on Lemosho (2008), I had mild AMS in the exact same spot as in 2000, descending into Barranco. As in 2000, I recovered completely overnight. The symptoms were much milder, probably because of our less strenuous itinerary. "

Meals are cooked and served by the support team in what seem very difficult conditions for preparation and cooking. However, most people find the food both palatable and plentiful. Longer expeditions sometimes arrange for a welcome re-supply of fresh food part way through the trip. Lunch stops may include hot food served at picnic tables: see below. The diet is rich in carbohydrates, good for helping to combat altitude symptoms. If you have dietary restrictions, allergies or any medical conditions, make sure you communicate them well ahead of time.

Bring some snacks such as dried fruit, trail mix, power bars or high energy food or gel. They will boost your energy and morale, and can be shared. On summit day, you may be hiking for 15-18 hours, and snacks help to bridge the long gaps between meals. Bring also some throat sweets or peppermints as many people suffer from dry throats at altitude.

Lunch stop below Lava Tower

Few people carry sufficient water, or keep it handy enough. When walking at altitude, you lose moisture with each breath, expiring warm moist air and inspiring cold dry air. Also altitude makes your body produce more urine (the diuretic effect), and you're losing water vapour all the time, especially when exercising, as invisible sweat. Expect to drink 2-4 litres per day on top of soup and other liquids you take with meals. Try to monitor the colour of your urine: pale straw colour is fine, but yellow warns that you are dehydrated.

Aim to drink before you become thirsty: a water bladder with tube is ideal as it lets you take sips whenever you need, without having to stop or fiddle with your rucksack. Water is safe to drink if it has been boiled (at any altitude) or purified with iodine. Boiling and cooling enough water for a large group can take ages, so it's worth carrying drops or tablets unless you are certain that you'll have plenty of safe water. Follow the iodine instructions about standing time and dosage, and if the flavour bothers you, use neutralising tablets or powder (e.g. Vitamin C).

You can limit your fluid loss through sweating by adjusting your clothing. Try to anticipate your body's heat production. Shed excess layers just before you start to overheat, and restore them just before you start to feel chilled (e.g. for a rest stop or because the weather changes). Aim to maintain a steady pace and wear clothes designed for flexibility. For example, choose a jacket with underarm zippers and large pockets, and trousers with zip-off legs.

Beyond the last water point, you have to carry all the water you need. On summit day, take good care of your water supply, keeping it well insulated and close to your body heat to prevent freezing. With bladder systems, the narrow tube is very prone to freeze, so either protect it or else after each sip blow back the water to keep the tube empty. Staying well hydrated helps the blood to circulate to your extremities, in addition to warding off AMS.

A decision to trek to extreme altitude carries risks for some people. Before you commit yourself, talk to your doctor. He or she may have no detailed knowledge of altitude physiology, so take along your proposed itinerary and route profile: see p16. With a sensible approach, most people can expect healthy side-effects from preparing for a Kili trip.

Check the latest information on which vaccinations are required and recommended for Tanzania, and over what timetable. Store your records safely: you may be refused entry without proof of yellow fever protection, for example.

Take advice about anti-malarial drugs and insect repellents, and follow it carefully. Malaria is a life-threatening disease which is easy to prevent but difficult to treat. You need protection, if only for the beginning and end of your trip. If you haven't taken anti-malarials before, ask whether you need to take a trial dose before leaving home. Some can cause side-effects, including nausea and other problems which could be confused with AMS symptoms. You might also want to discuss Diamox: see p24.

Remember to visit your dentist well before departure. Your feet are about to become the most important part of your body, so consider seeing a chiropodist, and obtain blister prevention and treatment. If you are a blood donor, make your last donation at least eight weeks before you leave. (Your blood probably won't be welcomed for at least a year after you return, as AIDS is endemic in this part of Africa.)

Upset digestion is not uncommon, so consider what remedies to take, including anti-diarrhoea medicine. Some of those who have to turn back do so because of digestive problems and consequent dehydration. The nature of the latrines and absence of running water in most campsites makes it crucial to keep yourself clean. Take a good supply of wet wipes, preferably medicated.

The equatorial sun is very strong, and its radiation more damaging at altitude, so sunburn is a serious risk. Bring a wide-brimmed sun hat, cover-up clothing and cream with a high Sun Protection Factor, at least SPF 35-45 for your face and lips. You need wrap-around sun-glasses or glacier glasses that block at least 99% of UV radiation, otherwise you risk the pain, headaches and double-vision of 'snow blindness' on summit day.

Contact lens wearers face extra problems at altitude. Even 'soft' lenses decrease the amount of oxygen available to the cornea. Removing and caring for contact lenses hygienically can be difficult on the mountain. Take spectacles (glasses) as back-up, in case the lenses become painful to wear.

Mobile phones

With a good signal almost everywhere on Kili, there's no reason (apart from consideration for your fellow hikers) why you can't phone home from the summit. However, don't promise to phone: failure would create needless anxiety. In extreme cold, battery life is very short and electronics sometimes die. Anyway, it may be too cold to take your gloves off, or your brains may be too scrambled to remember how to text or phone. If you plan to use a mobile a lot, it's much cheaper to buy a Tanzanian SIM card locally.

Advance planning checklist

This checklist may to help remind you what needs to be done, and when:

- consult medical advisor about your proposed trip
- take out suitable insurance as soon as you book
- check passport expiry date and apply for visa well in advance
- plan and carry out training programme for fitness and stamina

- check which inoculations and anti-malarials are needed
- visit dentist and/or chiropodist (foot specialist) for check-up
- learn some Swahili if possible
- weigh your kit and buy or borrow lightweight upgrades if need be
- blood donors: last donation no less than 8 weeks before departure.

Muscles get stronger if they are used regularly, at a suitable level and for a sustained period. This is known as the training effect. The heart is the most vital muscle to train, so that it can pump blood more efficiently and deliver more oxygen. Your cardiovascular (CV) system – your heart and lungs working together – is severely tested by climbing at altitude.

At sea level, most fit people have a low resting pulse and a high maximum heart rate. Depending on activity level, the heart might beat at any rate between 50 and 200 beats per minute (bpm). At altitude, the resting pulse increases and the maximum reduces, so you climb within a smaller range.

Awareness of heart rate and target zones can help to optimise your training programme. CV fitness improves if you exercise 3-6 times per week for at least half an hour with heart rate in your 'target zone', which is 70-85% of maximum heart rate. As your fitness improves, you have to work harder to push your heart into its target zone. Establishing your target zone and exercising within it is much easier if you use a heart rate monitor: see panel below.

People vary widely in their maximum heart rate. Discover your own by experiment if possible. Ignore the widespread tables of zones

Heart rate monitors

Monitors have two elements: on the left is a wrist-worn display of heart rate, to its right the chest-worn sensor. A monitor takes out the guesswork by telling you how hard your body is working. It can help on the mountain by monitoring your acclimatisation and helping you to avoid ascending too quickly by reminding you how fast your heart is beating. A basic monitor can cost as little as $25 (£15) and makes life easier than trying to feel your neck pulse while exercising. More advanced monitors let you set target zones, store performance data and design training programmes.

calculated by an age-related formula. They are unduly cautious for high-altitude trekking, being averaged out for general use. Establish the best target zone for you, given that on summit day your heart may have to work at 125-150 bpm for hours on end.

Without a monitor, work hard enough to make yourself pant, but not so hard that you can't also talk. For endurance, include much longer sessions at least once a week, to prepare your body for the long hours of sustained effort at altitude. Progressively build up both the duration and difficulty of the sessions.

There are training programmes of many kinds. Most people use hiking, running or cycling as their prime activity. Some experts advocate *cross training* and *interval training*. Cross training involves mixing in another form of exercise, e.g. if your core discipline is running, you might cross-train once a week by cycling or hill walking. Interval training means varying your effort level sharply every couple of minutes during a single session. You keep challenging your heart, helping to prepare yourself for the varying effort. Some experts argue for a rest day after every training session, others suggest resting one day a week.

Fitness, strength and stamina are all important for climbing Kili. Don't rely on a single form of exercise. The smooth surface of an indoor treadmill does nothing to prepare your leg muscles for climbing loose scree or rough, steep terrain, perhaps in a strong headwind. Try to include some brisk hill walking or cross-country jogging expeditions in the months and weeks prior to departure.

However you exercise, minimise the risk of straining your muscles by warming up slowly beforehand, cooling down gently afterwards, and stretching. Stretching beforehand reduces the risk of injury. Afterwards, it prevents a build-up of lactic acid in your muscles, leading to stiffness the day after. Drink plenty of water before, during and after your sessions.

If you are seriously overweight, don't contemplate climbing Kili. Surplus fat not only adds to your load, it also increases the demand for oxygen and is a risk factor for AMS. If you need to shed some fat, do it gradually and well ahead of your trip; your fitness training should help. Don't overdo the weight loss: most people lose some weight during the climb, and body fat insulates against the cold. Beware of hypothermia and of frostbite.

Start training well in advance. If you are already fit, a month of special effort might be enough, but if not, try to start 3-6 months in advance. If you smoke, give it up, at least until after your trip.

Stop training a day or two before you leave. If you have a spare day on arrival in Tanzania, go for a long walk. Moshi is a town of about 150,000 people, with a colourful ethnic and religious mix. Its fine mosque is next to the Hindu temple, with many Christian churches scattered around.

Mosque in central Moshi

The packing list on pp36-7 may look daunting, but you'll probably have much of the kit you need from previous hiking trips, notably a comfortable pair of **hiking boots**. Because of the very cold nights at altitude, a really warm **sleeping bag** is vital, rated to at least -18°C (0°F) and better if possible (or take a microfleece liner bag). A self-inflating **mattress** is needed on all routes except Marangu. If you can't afford to buy good ones, then borrow or hire: you can't enjoy your holiday if you are too cold to sleep well.

Err on the generous side when choosing your day **rucksack**: on summit day you need plenty of room for spare clothing. Side-pockets and D-rings are useful for keeping small stuff handy, and shock-cord lacing is great for drying off wet things on the outside. A normal or winter daypack holds 35-45 litres (about 1.5 cubic ft).

Even if you don't normally use **poles** when hiking, consider trying them before this trip. They improve your balance, save effort and reduce knee strain, especially on the steep descent. Telescopic poles can be set longer for downhill, shorter for uphill and stowed on your rucksack when scrambling. But be sure to try out anything you buy specially long before you set off. Kili is not the best place to learn to use poles properly.

Because of the extreme daily range of temperature, a layering system is needed to control your body temperature and sweating. The **base** should be a 'wicking' fabric, such as knitted polyester. Over that goes a medium-weight **fleece**. The outer layer consists of **breathable waterproofs** (jacket and trousers). Many people also take a down jacket, for wearing around camp at altitude. Good **gloves**, footwear and head/face protection are vital to avoid hypothermia and frostbite.

When hiking, everything that isn't in your backpack will be in your **kit bag**, which will be carried on a porter's head. Suitcases and rucksacks are unsuitable: the bag should be large, soft and waterproof, without a frame, wheels or dangling straps. Buy or borrow a holdall or kit/duffel bag – either tough enough to survive airplane baggage handling, or packed inside something which is. If your tour operator provides a kit bag, consider a luggage strap to make yours distinctive from the rest.

Long before you leave, do a trial pack to find out if your mountain kit is within target weight (normally 15kg/33lbs, but check with your operator). Work through the list omitting your hiking boots and anything else you are certain to be wearing. Discard excess packaging but organise your stuff for easy retrieval. Zip-lock polythene and mesh bags are great for keeping small stuff handy and visible, and cling-film keeps moisture off batteries and other delicate items. Time can be short on the mountain and if you are feeling unwell, finding things easily makes a big difference. Weigh your bag, and if it's too heavy, try again with reduced quantities.

For the journey, pack as hand baggage anything fragile (torches, sunglasses, camera) and any medicines you need during the flight. Hand baggage is also the place for passport, tickets, vaccination records, valuables and hiking boots (at least on the outward leg). Take a photocopy of your passport for use on trek. Remember the security rules about sharp items, fluids and pastes.

Luggage will be carried on a porter's head

Before you set off for the trek, split your stuff into three piles:

a) surplus kit and valuables to be left at your hotel, e.g. spare toiletries, a set of clean clothes, airplane reading and anything you need for excursions, safaris and other parts of your holiday

b) hiking kit for day one that you will either wear or carry in your rucksack (including waterproofs, camera gear, snacks, cash and plenty of water; also headtorch on Lemosho only): you'll have no access to your main kit bag before reaching camp

c) your mountain luggage (to weigh under 15kg including kit bag).

Porters' loads are weighed at the Park gates

1 Planning and preparation
Packing list

People vary widely, so this list won't suit everybody, but it's a starting-point.
Items in *italics* are ones we regard as optional rather than essential.
If you feel the cold badly, take more and warmer layers

Footwear	comfortable hiking boots	wear or pack as hand-baggage
	warm hiking socks	e.g. merino wool
	liner or lightweight socks	for lower altitudes
	blister protection	e.g. Compeed/Second Skin
	gaiters	to keep scree and mud out of boots
Hands	thin liner gloves	
	warm, windproof gloves/mittens	important on summit day
Trek clothing	thin hiking trousers	zip-off legs allow use as shorts
	base layer/thermal underwear	
	middle layer (tops and trousers)	
	warm fleece jacket	e.g. windblock
	waterproof/windproof outer layer	
	down jacket with hood	to wear around camp
Head/eyes/ lips/face	sun hat	wide brim for neck protection
	warm hat	wool or fleece
	sunglasses/glacier glasses	good UV protection needed
	balaclava(s)/face protection	ideally 1 silk, 1 fleece
	sunscreen and lip salve	SPF 35-55 if possible
	insect repellent	for lower altitudes
Trekking gear	water bladder or bottle	to hold at least 2 litres
	stainless steel thermos	for summit day
	water purification	e.g. iodine drops or tablets
	telescopic trekking poles (pair)	especially for steep descent
	wet wipes	use before touching food
	snacks and throat sweets	for dry throat at altitude
	toilet paper	biodegradable

Medical/	first aid kit including scissors,	aspirin/ibuprofen for headaches,
first aid	tweezers, plaster, medicines	Imodium for bowel arrest
	AMS relief/prevention	e.g. Diamox

Camping/sleeping

	warm sleeping bag	down-filled lighter than synthetic
	microfleece or silk bag liner	adds warmth/flexibility
	trek pillow	extra comfort
	self-inflating mattress	e.g. Therm-a-Rest (not needed for Marangu)
	headtorch and pocket torch	LED type saves batteries
	personal washing kit, trek towel	whatever toiletries your require
	camera, spare cards, spare batteries	battery life much shorter when cold
	trainers/hut slippers	for comfort in camp
	mobile phone	signal generally strong, but see p29
	guidebook, map, light reading,	
	cards, MP3 player, notebook, pen	whatever helps to pass time in camp

Rucksacks/packing

	kit bag	large, light, waterproof
	rucksack	35-45 litres ideal
	waterproof liners and/or covers	protection within kit bag/rucksack
	compression stuff-sacs	for all bulky items
	padlock	security for hotel cache

Other clothing

	cool, lightweight clothes and	for flight and pre-/post-trek; expect to cache
	sandals, swimwear etc.	at hotel

Travel documents

	passport with Tanzanian visa	must have 6+ months validity; take photocopy on trek
	air tickets	return flight may need to be reconfirmed
	insurance policy	check validity; bring 24-hr tel no
	credit cards	as backup; acceptable in hotels and some shops
	cash	US dollars needed for tips for guides and porters, and
		for soft drinks; take plenty of small notes (see p40)

At 950,000 sq km, Tanzania is a large country, over twice the area of California. Its tourist attractions including its Indian Ocean coastal resorts and islands, and game viewing. National parks and game reserves cover 14% of its area. In 2009 its population was about 41 million, with a life expectancy of only 52 years.

This is one of the world's poorest countries, although its GDP grew in 2007-08. About 80% of the workforce of nearly 20 million are subsistence farmers. Dar es Salaam is the main port and commercial capital, but Dodoma was designated as the new capital in 1974. Dodoma is located in a sparsely populated agricultural region and is the centre of Tanzania's nascent wine industry.

The four colours in the national flag symbolise its people (black), land (green), sea (blue) and mineral wealth (gold). Its motto *Uhuru na umoja* means 'freedom and unity' in Swahili, the national language: see p96. Tanganyika gained independence in 1961, and became the United Republic of Tanzania when it joined with Zanzibar in 1964. Julius Nyerere was its President from 1962-85.

Mount Kilimanjaro is an important national symbol of freedom (*uhuru*). The Uhuru Torch was first lit at its summit in 1961, in the words of Nyerere's famous speech, '[to] shine beyond our borders giving hope where there was despair, love where there was hate, and dignity where before there was only humiliation.'

In 1973, the whole mountain above the 2700m contour was declared a National Park and in 1989 Unesco listed it as a World Heritage Site. It's of huge economic importance to Tanzania, acting as a magnet to tourists and a major income stream. Each year, an estimated 25,000-30,000 tourists try to climb it. The fees to enter the Park average about $500-$750 per tourist per trip. That suggests an income of at least $15-20 million from this source alone.

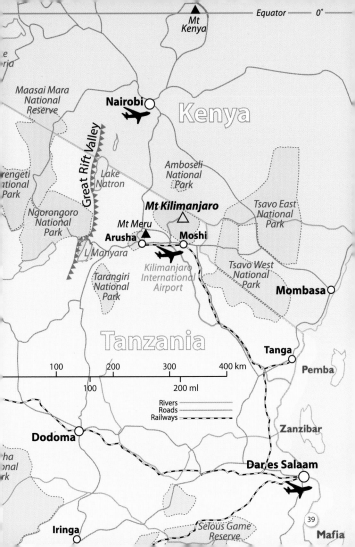

Kili is threatened by the scourge of woodcutters, poachers, fires and litter. We can help, not only by never leaving litter, but also by picking up the odd piece from the trail. Some guides carry a trash bag for this purpose. Each visitor's behaviour acts as an example, good or bad, to others.

The Tanzanians who live and work on Kili are Chagga, third largest of Tanzania's 120 tribal groups. They arrived several centuries ago but were nomadic at first, settling and farming from the 18th century onward. Mountain staff are self-employed, within a framework established by the Tanzanian National Parks, and they have a reputation for independence and strength of purpose.

Christianity was introduced here by Lutheran and Catholic missions during the 19th century, and Christian beliefs and practices have been integrated with tribal traditions. The Chagga have many legends and beliefs about the mountain, and their tradition is to bury their dead facing Kibo.

Currency

The official currency is the Tanzanian shilling (TZS), but US dollars are widely accepted in hotels, tourist outlets and on the mountain. The shilling is tiny: there were about 1000 to the dollar in 2005 and 1350 or so by 2009.

Bring lots of small dollar bills: this helps to divide the tip kitty, and also to avoid masses of TZS in change whenever you shop. Traveller's cheques are much less convenient, and useless on the mountain. Credit cards are accepted in many hotels and large shops. Cash machines are very sparse and don't work when there's a power cut, so it's better to bring what you need.

Bank opening hours are generally 08.30 to 16.00 on weekdays plus Saturday mornings. Offices keep similar hours, but often close between 12.00 and 14.00.

Time zone

Local time throughout Tanzania is three hours ahead of Greenwich Mean Time, eight hours ahead of New York. Daylight saving time does not apply.

Power supply

Mains electricity is about 240-250 volts AC, 50 Hz and there can be surges in or interruptions to the supply. Sockets and plugs vary in shape and style, often including European 2-pin round and/or British 3-pin square.

Telephone and internet

Telecom offices and internet cafés in Moshi and Arusha have long opening hours and charge much less than hotels. Depending on your mobile phone contract and usage, you may save large amounts by buying a new SIM card locally.

To dial Tanzania from your home country, prefix the Tanzanian number with +255. To dial home from Tanzania, dial 00 (or possibly 000) before your country code and number.

Ptolemy of Alexandria wrote of a 'great snow mountain' in the second century AD, and Kilimanjaro was mentioned by Chinese and Arab writers in the 12th and 13th centuries. However, Europeans were surprisingly slow to 'discover' and accept the idea of a snow-capped mountain only 3° south of the equator.

In 1848, missionary Johannes Rebmann, on an expedition to Kilimanjaro, observed 'something remarkably white on the top of a high mountain'. He soon realised that it was snow, and later identified the twin peaks of Kibo and Mawenzi. British armchair geographers refused to believe his first-hand account, published in April 1849 but not accepted for a further 12 years.

Serious attempts by Europeans to climb Kilimanjaro began in 1861, but most groups turned back at the snow-line, then as low as 4000m. In 1889, geology professor Hans Meyer and Austrian mountaineer Ludwig Purtscheller mounted a six-week expedition supported by a team of local Chagga porters and guide John Lauwo. Finally, on 6 October 1889 they reached the summit and named it Kaiser Wilhelm Spitze after the emperor of the time: the mountain then lay in German East Africa.

Contrary to a widespread myth, Kilimanjaro was not 'given' by Queen Victoria to Kaiser Wilhelm, her grandson. The reason that the border bends southward between the mountain and coast was to place the sea port of Mombasa in Kenya, then British. German East Africa kept the port of Dar es Salaam as part of the carve-up of Africa finally agreed by the European powers in Berlin in 1896.

Meyer returned to Kili in 1898, this time climbing only as far as the crater rim. He was shocked by the extent of the glaciers' retreat, and predicted that they would all be gone within 30 years: see also p45. It was a further 20 years before anybody followed Meyer to the summit, the next ascent being made by a surveyor called Lange in 1909. Three years later, Mawenzi was summited by climbers Edward

Oehler and Fritz Klute, whose surnames have left their marks on the Shira Plateau. They went on also to summit Kibo from the west. There had been only a handful of ascents by the time the Great War broke out in 1914.

After the war, ascents became more frequent, especially those of Lutheran pastor Richard Reusch, who from his home in Marangu climbed it over 40 times from 1926 onward. He was the one who found the frozen leopard later made famous by Ernest Hemingway, and the first to see into the crater which now bears his name.

By the 1930s, the era of exploration was giving way to the rise of tourism, with the building of Kibo Hut in 1932 being a landmark. Hotels in Marangu started running guided ascents, although numbers grew slowly at first. By 1959, about 700 visitors tried for the summit, of whom around 50% reached Gillman's Point.

Numbers increased rapidly in the 1990s, when tourism was increasing by about 12% each year and an attempt on Kili was becoming part of any adventurous tourist's goals while in eastern Africa. By the millennium about 20,000 visitors were climbing Kili each year. By 2009 the annual estimate was 25,000-30,000 and still rising. By the time you read this, it will be higher still.

Kili's summit can become crowded

The Great Rift Valley reached its present form only between 1 and 2 million years ago. Compared with the formation of the earth around 4000 million years ago, in geological terms this is very recent. Long before Kilimanjaro was formed there was a gently rolling plain with the remains of a few eroded mountains. About a million years ago, the plain buckled and slumped, sinking over a period to form a huge basin known as the Kilimanjaro Depression.

The Kilimanjaro of today was formed between 500,000 and 750,000 years ago from three volcanic centres: Kibo was, and still is, the highest at 5895m. It's connected by its Saddle region to Mawenzi (5149m). Shira, at 3962m, is the oldest and was the first to become extinct and collapse into a caldera about 500,000 years ago.

Eruptions and lava flow raised Kibo to a height of about 5900m some 450,000 years ago. Uhuru Peak, Kibo's 'summit', is the highest point of a giant oval crater rim more than 3 km long by 2 km wide. There is no single name for Kilimanjaro in Swahili: its two main peaks are called *Kipoo* (Kibo) and *Kimawenzi* (Mawenzi).

The Shira Plateau was later worn down by erosion, and volcanic minerals such as obsidian can still be found. Weathering exposed the jagged crags of Mawenzi, formed from slower-cooling, erosion-resistant rocks. Around 100,000 years ago, subsidence caused a huge landslide that breached part of Kibo's western crater rim, and scoured out the Great Barranco valley.

Kibo continued to be active, and even today it's technically dormant rather than extinct. Its most violent eruptions were around 350,000 years ago, producing lava flows up to 50m thick. Black lava filled in the Shira caldera and flowed over the Saddle area towards Mawenzi.

Later volcanic activity on Kibo formed many parasitic craters (small conical hills formed by offshoots of the main lava flow). These are obvious in the photograph on p81. Eruptions also created the

Reusch Crater, concentric with, and inside, the main crater. Over 200 years ago, the last volcanic puff formed the smaller Ash Pit inside the Reusch Crater. Traces of volcanic activity persist there, with hot sulphurous fumes, but very few tourists are able to go there.

Kilimanjaro's extraordinary scenery was formed not only by volcanic heat, but also by ice. The ebb and flow of the glaciers has modified the shape of the mountain over hundreds of thousands of years. In extreme glacial times, an unbroken sheet of ice covered the entire mountain down to about 4000m, with finger glaciers reaching down to the tree line at 3000m.

You might expect the sun's rays to melt the glaciers, but in fact the flat, white ice reflects most of the radiation. Instead, the dark lava and rocks absorb the heat, and the warmer ground undermines the ice cliffs above, creating undercuts and overhangs. As ice blocks fall off and columns splinter, they create shade that helps the ground

Snow-covered Reusch Crater (c. 1990)

to absorb further heat, melting more ice. You can hear the cracking sounds clearly if you walk past the summit glaciers in suitable conditions.

Sadly, Kibo is gradually losing its ice cap – over 80% has gone since it was first surveyed accurately in 1912. Although global warming probably has a role, geologists confirm that Kilimanjaro has a long history of glacial advance and retreat. At times it has been completely ice-free for tens of thousands of years, partly because of volcanic activity. At other times, the ice cover has been so complete that ascent by trekking would have been impossible.

A 2002 study from Ohio State University predicted that the glaciers will be gone by 2015-20. Five years later, a team from the University of Innsbruck said the main ice cap would be gone by 2040 but that some ice would persist on the slopes. Whatever the actual time-scale, it's important to enjoy the extraordinary beauty of the summit glaciers while we still can.

Kibo's glaciers are in retreat

Five habitat zones encircle the mountain, each for about 1000m of altitude and each with its own climate, plant life and animals. The higher you go, the colder it gets and the lower the rainfall, limiting the number of species. These conditions demand remarkable adaptations for survival.

Summit

High desert

Heath and moorland

Rain-forest

Lower slopes

6000m
19,680ft

5000m
16,400ft

4000m
13,120ft

3000m
9840ft

2000m
6560ft

The lower slopes

Between about 800 and 1800m, the Chagga people cultivate the rich volcanic soil for crops such as maize, coffee and bananas. The south and west sides of the mountain are wetter and more fertile, with rainfall varying from 500-1800mm per year.

There are brilliant wild flowers all around. Interesting vegetation supports a wide range of bird life, including the common bulbul (brown with a black crest), the tropical boubou (a black and white shrike), brown speckled mousebirds and nectar-feeding sunbirds (long curved bills and iridescent feathers).

You may see monkeys on the lower slopes, though they are commoner higher up, in the forest – 'blue monkeys' and colobus, see p87.

Banana palm in flower

Blue monkey

The rain forest occurs between about
1800-2800m, with rainfall of about 200cm
(79in) per annum on the southern slopes.
To the west and north is much drier, and on
the Rongai route the rain forest is a narrow
band. A band of clouds often forms, causing
mist and high humidity.

*Impatiens
kilimanjari*

Mosses and ferns flourish in these conditions, and grow to giant
size. Trees are decked with streamers of bearded lichen: see p74.
Wild flowers include violets, gladiolus, orchids and some *endemic*
species – found nowhere else in the world. One of the most delicate
is *impatiens kilimanjarii* – related to the 'busy Lizzie'.

Common trees include teak, camphorwood and the huge yellow-
woods or *Podocarpus*: see p62. An oddity is the lack of bamboo,
which occurs in the upper belt of rain forest elsewhere in East Africa.

Fruit trees attract many birds: if you hear a bird braying like a
donkey, it is probably a silver-cheeked hornbill. If you are lucky
enough to see a large bird flashing crimson at its wings, it could
be a turaco. Most animals are all too easily hidden in the thick
vegetation. You will likely see or hear more monkeys, which also
feast on fruit.

Protea kilimandscharica

Heath and moorland

Between 2800m and 4000m are overlapping zones of heath and moorland, with annual rainfall about 130cm (51in) lower down, reducing to 50cm higher up. Frost forms at night, and intense sunshine makes for high daytime temperatures.

Kniphofia thomsonii

Heather and allied shrubs are well adapted to these conditions. Tree heathers (*Erica arborea*) have tiny leaves and thick trunks, and grow 3m high, even taller in the forest below. *Protea kilimandscharica* is common here, but unique to the mountain: see p48. You may recognise red-hot pokers (*Kniphofia thomsonii*) standing as if in a garden at sea level.

The moorland has many giant groundsels, especially near water courses. The most striking is *Senecio kilimanjari*, which grows up to 6m tall: see p82. The smaller *Lobelia deckenii* (up to 3m) has a hollow stem and spiralling 'leaves' that close over at night. Look inside and you will see blue flowers sheltering.

Animal sightings are scarce. Tiny four-striped grass mice flourish around Horombo Huts and you'll see birds around most camps: the shy alpine chat (small, dusky brown) and white-necked raven (large scavengers, see p79). On the Shira Plateau you'll see signs and spoor of larger animals: footprints of buffalo, and perhaps eland or jackal. Your guide may even have seen lion.

Lobelia deckenii

The montane (high) desert zone stretches from 4000-5000m and has low precipitation, less than 25cm (10in) a year. Here mid-day temperatures burn at 35-40 °C, but deep wintry chill falls at night. Soil is scanty, and is affected by *solifluction*: when the ground freezes, it expands and flows, disturbing plant roots. Only the hardiest can survive.

Helichrysum

Lichens are a very old life form that fares well in these conditions. They don't need soil, but grow directly on rock. Lichens are not plants but small ecosystems, involving close partnership (*symbiosis*) between a fungus and algae (and sometimes bacteria, too). Fungi have no chlorophyll, so they rely on the algae for photosynthesis to provide it with nutrients. The fungus' role is to protect and supply moisture to the algae. Lichens are amazingly good at absorbing moisture from dew or fog – up to 35 times its body weight.

The desert is also relieved by *Helichrysum* – clumps of hardy, daisy-like flowers, also known as everlastings. They have a big altitude range, and you may have noticed them lower down. They tend to be more colourful at lower altitudes, especially when in bud: see p75. Higher up, they are usually either white or yellow.

Lichens store moisture from dew

Higher up, it's colder and drier still, and any precipitation (under 10cm a year) falls mainly as snow. This often condenses from clouds sucked up from below when air pressure drops because of the warming effect of the sun. There is no surface water: it disappears into porous rock or is locked in as ice and snow.

Living things must endure blazing equatorial sun by day and arctic conditions by night. Here altitude defies latitude. With deep frosts, fierce winds, scarce moisture and less than 50% of the oxygen available at sea level, the environment is deeply hostile to life of any kind.

Nevertheless, you may spot a few lichens, which grow very slowly at this height. Treasure any that you see: they may be among the oldest living things on earth. The highest flowering plant ever recorded was a small Helichrysum growing in the crater at 5670m.

Animal sightings are very unlikely, although wild dogs have been reported occasionally. In 1926 Donald Latham found and photographed the carcass of a leopard on the crater rim, 300m north of Gillman's Point, at a spot now known as Leopard Point. Hemingway immortalised this animal in his 1938 short story *The Snows of Kilimanjaro*, remarking that 'No one has explained what the leopard was seeking at that altitude'.

The Kersten glacier, seen from the crater rim

3·1 Why climb Mount Meru?

Mount Meru was created by the same volcanic activity as the Great Rift Valley. About 250,000 years ago a massive eruption tore out its eastern crater wall, leaving a huge horseshoe crater rising to 4566m (14,980ft). Its last eruption was in 1910, six years *after* the first recorded ascent to its summit by Franz Jaeger.

There are good reasons to make Meru a prelude to Kili:

- The expedition makes ideal acclimatisation just before tackling Kili, and the two mountains are only about 50km/31mi apart.
- It's Tanzania's second highest mountain, with some challenging terrain, fine scrambling and dramatic crater views. Summiting Meru will give you more confidence to tackle Kili.
- Arusha National Park is rich in wildlife, and far less busy than Kili, so you see many more animals.
- Meru provides valuable experience of the Tanzanian trekking routine and of organising your kit; even the 2 am start is good practice for Kili.

Little Meru
3820

Rhino Point
3800

Saddle
Huts
3570

Mgongo wa
tembo
3200

Miriakamba
Huts
2510

Ash Cone
3667

Kitot
Hill

Socialist
Peak
4566

Climbing Meru obviously adds to the cost and duration of your trip, although the daily cost is lower than Kili, and many outfitters offer discounts if you book the two together. If you can afford to include Meru, avoid the rainy season. The ascent includes a ridge walk (unsuitable if you get vertigo) and three stretches of exposed scrambling. In high wind, snow and/or ice, the terrain makes the crater hike even tougher, perhaps even unsafe, and you might have to settle for Rhino Point. However, your body would still benefit from Meru as a prelude to Kili.

Ignore three-day Meru itineraries: unless already acclimatised, you need four days. Starting from Momella Gate at 1500m, you sleep the first night at 2510m and the second at 3570m, then try for the summit at 4566m. Afterwards, descend only as far as Saddle Huts: you'll benefit from sleeping high and your summit day will be shorter. Many outfits expect you to descend to the lower hut, or even all the way to the Gate – thus losing 3000m of altitude just after you've summited! Confirm the itinerary in advance.

For optimum acclimatisation, set off for Kili straight after descending from Meru, though some groups prefer a full day's rest in between. You might even consider adding an extra night at Saddle Huts to make a five-day Meru trip.

Momella Gate
1500 G

Tululusia
Hill
2002

Arched
Fig Tree

4x4 route

Mt Meru
3·2 Momella Gate to Miriakamba Huts

Time (average)	**3-5 hours**
Altitude gained	**1010m (3310ft)**
Grade	**mostly easy, climbing steadily, with a few awkward parts**
Terrain	**park roads at first, then a good path punctuated by a few streams and rocks**
Summary	**pleasant ascent through varied scenery with plentiful chances of animal sightings and very few hikers**

To reach Momella Gate, you turn off the main Arusha/Moshi road near Usa River Village. This turn-out is about 20km from Arusha, 50km from Moshi and roughly 30km from Kilimanjaro Airport. After leaving the tarmac, you travel about 20km along a slow dirt road. Mostly this lies within the National Park, so be alert for animal sightings.

Your hike begins at Momella Gate, open 6.30 am to 6.30 pm, where Park fees must be paid and formalities completed, including weighing luggage and engaging porters. From there, we describe the northern route which is more direct than the southern, on a path that serves hikers only. The southern alternative is on a rough road which carries occasional 4x4 vehicles: this takes longer and is less suited to descent: see pp52-3. It features a giant arched fig tree, formed by aerial roots of the fig tree strangling its host tree

Starting across attractive open grassland, the northern path gains
height steadily, with good chances of seeing wildlife, so have your
binoculars handy: you are likely to see buffalo, bushbuck, giraffe,
warthog and zebra, and might be lucky enough to spot wandering
elephants. Because there are relatively few hikers, the animals are
not shy, and the Park Ranger who accompanies you carries a rifle in
case he should need to scare off elephant or buffalo.

You climb gently into lush green forest, with magnificent tall
trees decked with bearded lichens. Smaller trees include wild
honeysuckle, magnolia and brown olive, but look our also for
the mature giants which soar 25-35m above you: Yellow-wood
(*Podocarpus*), African Pencil Cedar and Strangler Fig. In the forest,
look out for colobus monkey and listen for the raucous shrieks of
the silver-cheeked hornbill. The electronic glassy cries are made by
the tropical bulbul, and stand out clearly from the birdsong of up to
400 other species.

After a pleasant uphill hike, you reach Miriakamba Huts. These
timber buildings stand in a grassy glade in the forest, the two
dormitory-style bunkhouses sleeping about 40 hikers each, with a
separate toilet block. There is provision for cooking (groups bring
their own equipment) and a good supply of water nearby. The setting is picturesque, with great views of Meru's sharp ridge towering
over you to the west and, distant to the east, toward Kili.

Miriakamba Huts, with Meru on its left

Time (average)	**3½-5 hours**
Altitude gained	**1060m (3480ft)**
Grade	**mainly moderate, climbing steadily and, in places, steeply**
Terrain	**path with mainly good surface, with some steep stony parts**
Summary	**a pleasant ascent through forest at first, with wider views opening out over the moorland above**

Leave Miriakamba early, aiming to complete this ascent by lunchtime so that your afternoon is free for rest or to ascend Little Meru (see below). At first you walk through luscious green forest, still with tall trees and colourful wild flowers. Bird life is still abundant, but you are unlikely to see large animals, although you will find buffalo and elephant spoor. After a couple of hours, you will reach a viewpoint named in honour of the elephants – *Mgongo wa tembo* or Elephant Ridge – marking your half-way point. Pause to enjoy the views over Meru's vast crater floor spread out below you, and look up to its dramatic summit ridge to the west.

Little Meru ▲- -
3820

Miriakamba
Huts
2510

Elephant Ridge 3200

Saddle
Huts
3570

The path continues its steep climb, the forest giving way to the tree heathers of the moorland, punctuated by colourful splashes of wild flowers. Your goal is the wide saddle or col between the shoulder of Mount Meru and its smaller sibling to the north, Little Meru.

After a couple of hours of steady ascent from Elephant Ridge, you reach Saddle Huts. The two bunkhouses, unlike Miriakamba's, are divided into eight rooms, housing four hikers to a room. There are a couple of toilets and water is

From Elephant Ridge

available from a stream ten minutes away. Stock up with plenty of drinking water for the long day tomorrow.

Little Meru

Unless you need an entire afternoon's rest before the long summit day, there is much to be said for climbing the shapely peak of Little Meru in the late afternoon. This modest climb (gaining a further 250m of altitude) helps with acclimatisation, and if you are lucky with the weather, the summit views are superb. Allow an hour or more for the ascent up a stony path, and about 45 minutes for descent. The summit has a cairn and sign proclaiming its name and height. The views towards Rhino Point and Meru's summit ridge will help you to anticipate the next day's ascent route, and towards sunset, the light can be sensational.

Time (average)	**ascent 5-7 hours plus descent 3-5 hours**
Altitude gained	**996m (3270ft)**
Grade	**moderate to steep, and very steep in places**
Terrain	**a mixture of scree and rocks, with three extended and exposed scrambles**
Summary	**a strenuous day, especially for hikers who find scrambling tiring; the reward is one of Africa's finest views**

Don't underestimate this mountain: although the altitude is less extreme, the terrain makes Meru's summit day tougher than Kili's. In good conditions, the climb is exhilarating and well rewarded by dramatic views, but in icy or windy conditions the terrain can be (literally) lethal, and you may have to settle for Rhino Point (3800m) instead. If that seems likely, defer your departure until 5 am or later, so as to benefit from sunrise over Rhino Point.

Most groups leave Saddle Huts at about 2 am. Ensure you have fresh batteries in your headtorch and take plenty of water and energy snacks. You begin with an hour's steep climb to Rhino Point. From there you drop downwards before scrambling across rocks and climbing steeply towards the crater rim. You then follow the narrow path all the way to the summit at 4566m.

Dramatic crater rim;
inset, Kili seen from Meru

Saddle Huts 3570 ▲Rhino Point 3800   Cobra Point 4350 ▲   Socialist Peak △ 4566

The next landmark is Cobra Point which, despite its altitude gain of 780m from Saddle Hut, is only about half-way in terms of time. Here you may enjoy amazing views of the 1500m cliff walls of the inner crater with its impressive ash cone. A short rest is in order: from here on, you follow the rim as it climbs tortuously for a further 212m, with various false summits separated by undulations and rock scrambles. The ridge is very narrow in places, with sheer drops on either side, and in high winds it is downright dangerous. The route is marked by splashes of green paint: follow these closely across the exposed rocky sections.

The sting is in the tail. The final approach is the toughest rock scramble yet, not helped by muscle fatigue and altitude. When you finally reach the metal Tanzanian flag, you've earned the amazing views. Despite its prosaic name (Socialist Peak), Meru boasts one of the finest panoramas in Africa. To the north-east, Rhino Point stands in front of Little Meru, while further east Kili's two peaks (Kibo and Mawenzi) float on the clouds, with Meru's dramatic crater in the foreground. To the south lies the vast Maasai plain, and to the west the vast Serengeti with the Great Rift Valley. To the north, the view is punctuated by volcanic upstarts: Lengai to the north-west, Longido due north and Namanga just to its east.

East over the Ash Cone

3·5 The descent

Even in good conditions, the descent is tiring, involving further scrambling and some ascent. It takes about 3-5 hours to descend to Saddle Huts. If you're descending to Miriakamba (a drop of 2052m/6730ft), allow at least another 2-3 hours.

You may find the daylight of your descent a mixed blessing: if you found scrambling in the dark challenging, you may not welcome seeing the extent of the exposure. As long as conditions remain good, there is nothing difficult for experienced scramblers, but take great care on the way down: remember that's when most accidents happen. Take your time, especially on the scrambling sections near the summit, around Cobra Point and approaching Rhino Point. Take time also to enjoy and perhaps to photograph the spectacular views, especially the parts that you ascended in darkness.

If you are overnighting at Saddle Huts, you'll relish the prospect of a long rest before the 2070m descent next day. If you must descend to Miriakamba on summit day, don't delay or you'll risk running out of daylight. Either way, it's a long hard day.

Looking down from the crater rim

Your final day's descent is the 1010m/3310ft from Miriakamba to Momella Gate. With the pressure off, you can enjoy this wonderful descent through the lush vegetation, with birdsong and possible animal sightings.

Before leaving Arusha National Park for your return drive, if you've time, make a small diversion to visit the dramatic waterfall near the Gate. Here the Tululusia River drops abruptly into a near-vertical rocky gorge, and you can go up to, and even stand behind, its splendid waterfall – an ideal cooling shower.

Crater rim descent

Descending to Miriakamba

Time (average)	**5-7 hours**
Altitude gained	**1200m (3940ft)**
Grade	**long climb with gentle gradients at first, increasing later**
Terrain	**muddy path with tree roots; very slippery when wet**
Summary	**a strenuous first day, tougher if wet underfoot, on an attractive path surrounded by rain forest**

After everybody's kit has been loaded, you are driven to Machame Gate to complete National Park formalities such as registering passport numbers and paying fees. From Moshi, the drive takes about 40 minutes, bringing you direct to altitude 1800m (5900ft). On the way, look out for crops such as bananas, maize and coffee, and also for exotic flowers and butterflies.

Formalities can take an hour or more, depending on the queues and your group size. If you meet your guides and porters before setting off, try to remember their names and faces: they're vital members of your team for the trip. Before setting off, make sure you have enough drinking water for the day and a packed lunch.

The walk through the rain forest is full of interest, with giant trees, wild flowers and tropical birds. Go slowly (*pole pole*) on this first day and drink lots of water to help with acclimatisation. The trail starts as a broad, winding 4x4 track which gives out after about 45 minutes.

Weeping yellowwood (podocarpus gracilior)

Machame
Gate
1800
G

Machame
Camp
3000

The path narrows and steepens, and after a futher hour or two you will reach clearings which are popular as lunch stops.

Mist and cloud are common in the middle of the day, and on arrival at Machame Camp you may see little. At this altitude, clear views are more likely in the early mornings. Get in the habit of looking around the campsite on arrival, and locate your headtorch long before darkness falls. In the morning, rise early and expect to pack your kit before breakfast.

Gladiolus natalensis

Machame Camp, early morning

Time (average)	**5-7 hours**
Altitude gained	**850m (2790ft)**
Grade	**generally steep climb with short scramble (about 8m vertical) to the plateau; gradients ease a bit afterwards**
Terrain	**surfaces mostly firm with only one real scramble, up the rocky ridge leading to the plateau**
Summary	**steady climb leads to a splendid campsite with fine views**

Scrambling up to Shira plateau

Machame Camp 3000

New Shira Camp 3850

After an early breakfast, you set off toward the Shira Plateau. Leaving the forest, the path heads up into the moorland along a ridge of volcanic rock. About two hours after Machame Camp, there is a short scramble up a rock 'wall', but this is neither difficult (American Class 3, British grade 1) nor high. The path climbs steadily along the ridge towards a picnic lunch stop, usually at about 3600m.

Once atop the rocky ridge, you head north-west, seemingly away from Kibo. After crossing some streams, you emerge on to the Shira Plateau, where the gradients ease at last. Shira is the oldest of the three volcanoes that make up the Kilimanjaro massif, the plateau being its *caldera* (collapsed crater). You'll see many volcanic features and minerals, including shiny black pebbles of obsidian.

Continuing north, you soon reach New Shira Camp, close to the Shira Caves. From here you may have splendid views of the Shira Ridge to the west, similar to the views shown on pp74-5. Looking east, you may see Kibo's Western Breach and glaciers. Far away, to the south-west, you might even glimpse Mount Meru.

Kibo, seen across the Shira Plateau

Time (average)	**5–6 hours**
Altitude gained	**rising 680m (2230ft) above New Shira before the steep descent to camp (100m/330ft net gain)**
Grade	**generally a steady climb, with some steep sections**
Terrain	**fairly rough path with some scree**
Summary	**through rocky semi-desert with dramatic views of the Lava Tower and Breach Wall**

After New Shira, the route turns sharply east, and at last you're walking toward Kibo and its Western Breach. The line of nearby hills to the left is the Oehler Ridge. There are impressive cliffs and rock formations all the way, with some interesting colours if the light is good. You climb steadily up a ridge and at about 4400m you may notice the Lemosho route joining you from the left (west).

About 500m afterwards, there's a junction where most groups divert uphill to Lava Tower (4600m) for extra acclimatisation. Some will want to scramble up this rock: see p67. Meanwhile, the porters follow the main trail downhill toward the Great Barranco.

The last few hours are a steep descent into the Barranco (valley), ending at altitude 3950m. Barranco Camp has a spectacular situation, below the Western Breach. Near sunset, the light on its rocks and ice can be magical: see front cover.

Senecio with Kibo behind

New Shira
Camp
3850

Lava Tower
4600

Barranco
Camp
3950

*Lava Tower from
the south: it can
be climbed by
scrambling up
its northern face,
with superb views
from the summit*

Time (average)	**7–9 hours**
Altitude gained	**rises 380m (1250ft) over the Barranco Wall, then falls and rises to Barafu (650m/2130 ft net gain)**
Grade	**after a stiff, exposed climb up the Barranco Wall, gradients ease**
Terrain	**mostly rocky with some scrambling needed**
Summary	**a taxing day, to be followed by an even tougher night, but with good views**

From the campsite, you head north for a short distance and cross a river before tackling the day's main challenge: the Barranco Wall. Although it looks nearly vertical, your route zigzags up it, and isn't nearly as hard as it first appears. The scrambling amounts to a stiff climb of over 300m (985ft) and could take 1-2 hours.

If you lack confidence while scrambling, follow someone who is experienced, putting your hands where he or she does: your feet will follow. If you are worried by the exposure, don't look down. Think of the Wall as a long, uneven staircase with handholds. It's amazing to watch the porters calmly walk up carrying heavy weights on their heads, hands in pockets.

Ascending the Barranco Wall

Barranco
Camp
3950

Barranco Wall

Karanga
Camp
4050

Barafu Camp
4600

After the Wall, the path crosses a plateau area divided by several valleys with superb views toward the southern icefields – the Heim, Kersten and Decken glaciers. You descend fairly steeply into the Karanga Valley (4000m). Some groups camp here, whereas others just make a lunch stop, important fuel for their night-time summit attempt. This being the last water point, before leaving Karanga all groups need to carry water from here to Barafu and beyond.

From the Karanga Valley, the path heads up diagonally towards Barafu Camp, seen on a ridge high above. Once you are settled into your camp, watch out for lovely evening light on Mawenzi. Kosovo is a small camp about an hour above Barafu, and much quieter; using it shortens the long summit day but needs special permission and may cost extra.

Both campsites are exposed and rocky, so familiarise yourself with the terrain before dark falls. Camp accidents happen mainly at night. Make sure that you have plenty of drinkable water for the climb. Put fresh batteries in your camera, and check your headtorch. Pack enough snacks to see you through the night climb, and arrange your warmest clothing, including handwarmers, gloves, hat and thermals. Then put your head down and sleep if you can.

Karanga campsite, with Kibo behind

Time (average)	**6–10 hours**
Altitude gained	**1295m (4250ft) to Uhuru**
Grade	**relentlessly steep ascent to crater rim, then undulating more gradually to Uhuru**
Terrain	**mixture of scree and rocks to Stella Point; perhaps snow**
Summary	**the most strenuous stage of a tough route, normally attempted between midnight and dawn**

You'll be woken around midnight to climb through the night. You need the early start to reach the summit and still have time to descend in daylight. From Barafu, you must gain 1295m of vertical height (from Kosovo, 1095m) to reach Uhuru. On the same day, you face a massive descent to Mweka Camp: see p93.

On waking, put on as much warm clothing as possible. To start with, you will be cold, perhaps very cold if it's windy, but you may need to shed layers after you've started climbing hard. Be sure to keep your extremities warm and make sure your water has not frozen. Drinking plenty is important for avoiding frostbite, as well as for acclimatisation.

Approaching Stella Point, past the Rebmann glacier

Barafu
Camp
4600

Kosovo
4800

Stella Point 5750 ▲

Uhuru
Peak
5895

The climb to Stella Point is by far the most daunting section of the Machame route. You face a combination of altitude and darkness with a long, steep slog up the scree and rock. The gradient increases as you approach the crater rim. If you persist, and escape altitude sickness, you will get there in the end. If your feet slip back on the scree, push harder on your poles and use upper body strength to haul yourself up. The guides don't use poles, but edge in with their boots. As you approach or reach Stella Point, the sunrise will raise your morale and body temperature: see the photograph on p84.

From Stella Point it takes another 45 minutes or so to Uhuru. Although the gradients are gentler and terrain easier, there are several false summits on the way. Be sure to reserve some energy for the descent: see p93. Meanwhile, you may find that reaching the summit gives you a rush of energy that sees you through this, perhaps the longest day of your life.

Guide descending from Uhuru

Time (average)	**2–3 hours**
Altitude gained	**400m (1310ft)**
Grade	**mostly a steady ascent, with some steep undulations**
Terrain	**narrow path enclosed by rain forest, slippery in wet weather**
Summary	**a short hike with some steep sections and lots of interest with wild flowers, birdsong and traces of large animals**

The Lemosho route starts from the west and offers a more scenic, less busy approach to Barranco Camp than the Machame route with which it merges. It gained fame in 2009 in the UK when televised on BBC1 as the route used by the Red Nose Climb stars. It spreads the hike to Barranco over 4 days, and with the optional overnight at Karanga, an 8-day Lemosho allows 6 days to reach Barafu – 33% longer than a 6-day Machame. Even a 7-day Lemosho itinerary has acclimatisation advantages.

Most of the first day is spent being driven, first to Londorossi Gate (2250m) to complete formalities. With fertile volcanic soil and generous rainfall, you'll notice fine crops of bananas, sunflowers, coffee and maize on the journey west. From Moshi, the 80-km drive takes about two hours on variable roads, perhaps extended by a stop to buy food. Then there's the protracted waiting while permits are issued and fees paid at the Gate, though a picnic lunch may help to pass the time.

Londorossi Gate

Lemosho
trailhead
2350

Big Tree
Camp
2750

From the Gate, the rough 4x4 track heads south to Lemosho Glades. In wet conditions this journey can be tough for both driver and passengers. By the time that the porters' loads have been divided and the guides are ready for you to set off, it may be late afternoon before you leave the trailhead at 2350m. Carry plenty of water and your head torch in case of arrival after dark.

Steep terrain with tree roots

The trail winds up through luxuriant rain forest, with huge trees bedecked with bearded lichen. The trail has lots of tree roots and may be slick with mud. There are steep undulations, especially at first, but the gradient slackens after a while. The sight of monkeys (blue and colobus), sounds of birds and profusion of wild flowers makes for plenty of interest. After a couple of hours, you reach Big Tree Camp (*Mti Mkubwa*). The Park authorities call it Forest Camp, but everybody else uses the obvious name.

Big Tree Camp

Time (average)	**4–6 hours**
Altitude gained	**750m (2460ft)**
Grade	**easy gradients at first, then steeper when climbing Shira Ridge**
Terrain	**mainly firm footing on good moorland paths with some rocky parts**
Summary	**a longer day with a telling altitude gain; plants, wild flowers and splendid wide views**

The day begins with easy, undulating walking through rain forest rich in wild flowers, its trees streamed with bearded lichen. Within an hour or so, there's an abrupt transition to boulder-studded moorland. You'll see tree heathers and many varieties of Helichrysum.

After a further hour or so, the long climb to the plateau begins in earnest: take your time and drink plenty of water. Today's altitude gain is nearly double yesterday's, not to be rushed. Your picnic lunch stop may be in a clearing among the giant heathers.

Bearded lichen

South over the Shira Plateau

The path finally levels out as you skirt the northern end of the Shira Ridge, which defines the western rim of the Shira Plateau. As you crest the rise, if it's not too cloudy, a panorama opens up over the rolling plateau, with its landmarks ahead – East Shira Hill, Shira Cathedral and Shira Needle, with Cone Place to the right: see below.

Impressive though the Shira peaks may look, they don't compare with the awesome massif of Kibo, distant in the south-east. Depending on your state of mind, you may find this glimpse of the task ahead inspiring or daunting. From the ridge, there's a short, pleasant descent to Shira 1 by a path through the boulders and masses more Helichrysum.

Helichrysum in bud, above Big Tree Camp

Time (average)	spread over two days, could take from 7-12 hours walking
Altitude gained	450m (1480ft) net gain, but Lava Tower is at 4600m (15,090ft)
Grade	easy to moderate, but steep descent from Lava Tower
Terrain	mainly firm paths with some rocky sections
Summary	two days spent exploring the fascinating Shira Plateau, with many options and lots of variety, a great prelude to the serious climb from Barranco

It takes two days to hike from Shira 1 to Barranco. There's a wide choice of intermediate campsites with confusingly similar names. From Shira 1 you may head for Shira Hut/Shira 2 (3850m), or Fischer (3930m) or stop for lunch at Fischer *en route* to camp at Moir Hut (4150m). (These camps lie north and north-east of New Shira as used by Machame.) The altitude gain from Shira 1 might be anything from 400m to 650m, but much less than yesterday's.

The hike features gentle ascent across the plateau, with the attraction of constant views of Kibo and its glaciers if the weather is clear. After 4km, the 4x4 track from Londorossi Gate (used mainly for emergency evacuation) joins from the left. You'll soon see Simba Cave picnic site (*simba* means lion) with an attractive pool nearby.

Rock pool near Simba Cave

Shira 1
3500

Fischer
3930

Moir
4150

Lava Tower
4600 ▲

Barranco
3950

Shira Hut 3900

The trail divides 1.5km after Simba Cave, where you'll either bear left for Fischer and Moir Camps or right for Shira Hut. Moir Camp has a fine situation, framed by the Lent group and with good views of Kibo to the right, beyond the Oehler Ridge.

Near Fischer Camp

The next day's destination is Barranco (3950m) with negligible altitude gain (perhaps even loss) – great for acclimatisation. The trails from the three campsites head south or south-east, and converge at about 4300m. Shortly you pass the grave of a Canadian hiker who was taken ill with AMS at Barranco and died before he could be evacuated. This is a sobering reminder of the importance of taking care – both of yourself and of other team members.

Within 1 km, at 4400m the Machame trail rises to join you along a ridge from the right (south-west), and 500m later there's a further junction. Some groups go direct from this trail junction almost south toward Barranco, but many opt for extra acclimatisation with an excursion to the dramatic Lava Tower (4600m): see photo on p67. Either way, from Barranco the Lemosho route is identical to Machame: see pp68-71.

Moir Camp

Time (average)	**3–4 hours**
Altitude gained	**800m (2625ft)**
Grade	**moderate ascent at first, steeper on approach to Mandara Huts**
Terrain	**mainly firm path, but may be muddy and slippery in wet weather**
Summary	**not strenuous, except in wet weather, but a significant altitude gain; rain forest full of fine trees, birdsong and wild flowers**

After your kit has been loaded, you'll be driven to Marangu Gate. From Moshi, the drive takes about 45 minutes, bringing you to altitude 1900m (6235ft). Marangu hosts the Headquarters of the National Park, and tends to be very busy. The formalities must be completed here (registering passport numbers and paying fees). Expect this to take an hour or two, depending on the queues and your group size: if you are lucky, it may be less.

Try to identify birds, flowers and trees to help pass the time. Also, make sure you have plenty of drinking water for the day, and a packed lunch. There's a monument to Hans Meyer's first ascent in 1889: see p41. If you meet your guides and porters before setting off, try to remember their names and faces. They're vital members of your team for the whole trip.

Marangu
Gate
1900
G

Kisambioni
2100

Mandara
Huts
2700

Beyond the gate, an archway on the left marks the start of the walkers' path. The broad 4x4 track straight ahead is the old hiking route, nowadays used only by porters and Park staff. Hikers take a narrower, more intimate trail that runs parallel. Both routes head northward and steadily uphill. Unless it's wet and slippery, this walk may seem disarmingly easy. It's hard to credit the altitude in such lush rain forest, but walk slowly (*pole pole*) and drink plenty of water to help your body to acclimatise.

After an hour or so, the trail runs alongside a stream. After you cross it by a bridge, there's a path junction where you might turn right across a wooden bridge to Kisambioni, near the 4x4 track. Although at 2100m it's less than halfway, the setting is attractive for a picnic lunch. Or, if you made an early start, you may postpone lunch until arrival.

The trail steepens as you approach Mandara Huts, where you will arrive early to mid-afternoon with plenty of time to settle in. The facilities include solar-powered lighting and flush toilets, with sleeping accomodation for 60 walkers, six to a hut. If possible, visit Maundi Crater, just above Mandara, and a short walk to its north-east. The small extra effort is rewarded by brilliant wild flowers and perhaps superb views of Kibo and Mawenzi.

*Mandara Huts;
white-necked
raven (inset)*

79

4
Mandara Huts to Horombo Huts

Time (average)	**5–7 hours**
Altitude gained	**1000m (3280ft)**
Grade	**steady climb at first, steeper undulations on approach to Horombo**
Terrain	**good firm path, making it easy to find your stride**
Summary	**a major altitude gain, but on easy terrain, and some inspiring views of the task ahead**

After an early start, the walk starts emerging from the forest. Soon, you'll see the parasitic cone of Kifinika Hill ahead on your left. You'll also gain intermittent views of Mawenzi (ahead to your right) and Kibo (distant ahead). The vegetation changes markedly, almost abruptly, from forest to tree heathers and moorland.

The picnic lunch stop is usually *Kambi Ya Taabu* – well over halfway at about 3400m (11,155ft). Here you may notice four-striped grass mice, which are keen, skilful scavengers, as are the huge white-necked ravens.

You'll probably arrive at Horombo by early to mid-afternoon and be allocated to huts as at Mandara. Horombo is very busy because ascending hikers spend two nights here, and it's also the overnight stop for descending hikers. Your second night will probably in the same hut, but leave your gear stowed tidily, just in case. Dinner, as at Mandara, is served in the communal dining hut by the support team.

Horombo Huts

Mandara
Huts
2700

Kambi
Ya Taabu
3400

Horombo
Huts
3700

Saddle
Walk

On your acclimatisation day, the trail north is highly recommended, known as the Upper Marangu Route or Saddle Walk. From the vast, bleak saddle between Kibo and Mawenzi, it offers terrific views of the task ahead: see photograph below. Anyway, the extra ascent (of up to 700m) is good acclimatisation. It's best to set off early, with less chance of showers and have the afternoon free to rest.

You'll also see Middle Red, West Lava and East Lava Hills, as well as Barafu Hut to the west. En route, you can visit Zebra Rocks, only 2km above Horombo and impressively stripey. Minerals seeping down the rock face have left pale vertical stripes against the dark lava.

Saddle area: the route to Gillman's Point is shown in yellow

Time (average)	**5–7 hours**
Altitude gained	**1000m (3280ft)**
Grade	**steepish climb at first, easing across the Saddle, then steeper again approaching Kibo Hut**
Terrain	**good path across the barren wastes of the Saddle region**
Summary	**another serious altitude gain, but on easy terrain, with good views of Mawenzi and Kibo**

You set off north-westerly from Horombo. At first, giant groundsel persist wherever there is a watercourse. Top up your water supplies at the Last Water point: it's about 400m vertical above Horombo Hut, with picnic tables. You are entering the high desert of the Saddle region, swept by howling winds and occasionally dusted in snow.

You pass Middle Red Hill on your right, then the Triplets (three parasitic cones) on the left. The path steepens, vegetation disappears and the landscape becomes bleaker still. Most people arrive at Kibo Hut with mixed feelings – of relief and anticipation.

Giant senecios above Horombo

Horombo
Huts
3700

Last
Water
4100 ▲

Kibo
Hut
4700

Try to spend the rest of the afternoon at Kibo resting before the midnight summit attempt. Your team may supply you with boiled water, but if not, be sure to purify plenty of drinking water for the night's walk. Pack it so your body warmth prevents it from freezing. The commonest mistake people make at altitude is not drinking enough.

Route junction with white-necked raven

This is also the moment to insert fresh batteries and perhaps a new card or film in your camera and to check your headtorch battery. Pack enough snacks to boost your morale through the night's walking, arrange your warmest clothing ready for action, including gloves, hat and thermals. Then put your head down and sleep if you can. If not, relax and think peaceful thoughts: you need rest before the very strenuous 24 hours ahead.

East from the Saddle toward Mawenzi

Time (average)	**6–10 hours**
Altitude gained	**1195m (3920ft)**
Grade	**moderate as far as Hans Meyer Cave, then very steep to Gillman's Point, with lesser gradients around the crater rim**
Terrain	**mainly scree (loose unless frozen) to Gillman's Point; then rocky path, perhaps with snow**
Summary	**by far the most strenuous stage, normally tackled overnight**

Most groups leave Kibo between midnight and 2 am to climb through the night. This is mainly so as to reach the summit around sunrise or soon after, with plenty of time to descend in daylight. From Kibo Hut you must gain 1195m of altitude to reach Uhuru, only to descend 2195m to Horombo: see p93. At night, the ascent may be easier since the scree might be frozen, and any snow should be less slushy in the early morning.

On waking, put on all your layers of clothing, and eat and drink whatever is available. Before setting off, check that your snacks are handy, and protect your drinking water from freezing. If using a headtorch, take care not to dazzle others by looking at them directly. At first you will be cold, perhaps very cold, and it may be difficult to keep your extremities warm enough. Soon you may be warm enough to shed layers, depending on your pace and the wind. The first half of the ascent is on an uphill, winding rocky path,

Sunrise behind Mawenzi, summit day

Hans Meyer Cave
5150

Gillman's Point
5695

Kibo Hut
4700

Uhuru
Peak
5895

and the guides normally set a very slow, rhythmic pace. After a few hours, you reach Hans Meyer Cave. Nearly half-way to Gillman's Point in altitude (450 of the 985m), it's rather less in terms of time. Still, it's a good place to rest before the most difficult section.

After the Cave, the path becomes steeper as it zigzags up through loose scree towards Gillman's Point. Your goal seems mysteriously to recede as you try to approach it. Simply plod on and you will get there in the end. By about 6 am, the sunrise over Mawenzi will raise your morale and body temperature, and once you reach Gillman's Point, the hardest part is over.

It takes another 1½ to 2 hours to achieve the final 210m of altitude to Uhuru. The gradients are gentler and terrain easier around the crater rim. Just under halfway, you pass Stella Point where you may be joined by Machame climbers. Be prepared for several false summits *en route*. Your sense of achievement at the summit may give you a rush of energy or even euphoria, but be sure to keep enough in reserve for the descent: see pp93-5.

Summit glacier seen from crater rim

Time (average)	**3–5 hours**
Altitude gained	**700m (2300ft)**
Grade	**mostly easy, with slightly steeper moorland section**
Terrain	**good path with no difficulties**
Summary	**a delightfully gentle first day, with great views over the plains of Kenya to the north and towards Kibo**

From Moshi, you will be driven anti-clockwise around the base of the Kili massif for about four hours, mainly on a rough dirt road passing through scattered Chagga villages. You'll probably stop at Marangu Gate *en route* to deal with Park formalities. Reaching the village of Tarekea, the road approaches and runs alongside the Kenyan border. Finally, 10km later, you arrive at the shanty village of Naremoru (1950m) and can begin your hike.

Rongai and other names

The Rongai route has many names: trail signage refers to Nalemuru or Naremoru, after the village at its foot, or the river that the trail criss-crosses. Older maps show Loitokitok (after a nearby Kenyan village) or Outward Bound (after the school movement that once used it). The original route started further north at Rongai village, but was closed once the improved route was developed and became known as Rongai.

Over Naremoru village

Naremoru
Gate
1950
G
Simba
Camp
2650

It starts with lush plantations of maize and potatoes, interspersed with pine saplings. You pass a sawmill where timber is processed. The shacks are used by tenant families who depend on subsistence farming. Higher up, the path goes through a band of rain forest, rich in exotic bird life. Here you may also hear or see troupes of colobus monkeys. Soon you reach an official rest stop with picnic table and toilet.

Colobus monkeys

Before long, the trees thin out and give way to open moorland, studded with wild flowers. The low rainfall limits the rain forest on these northern slopes, but you'll see much more of it on your descent. The path threads its way more steeply among the tree heathers, with wide open views over the plains of Kenya behind you. Soon you reach Simba Camp, with its secluded pitches: see p88. There are views of rounded Kibo to your right and jagged Mawenzi to your left, and fresh water from the Nare Moru river nearby.

View north from below Simba Camp

Time (average)	**5–8 hours**
Altitude gained	**1250m (4100ft)**
Grade	**mostly easy, with some moderately steep sections**
Terrain	**good path, with no technical difficulties**
Summary	**a straightforward hike with very large altitude gain; can be split into two days at Second Cave, which is also where direct and indirect routes diverge**

From Simba Camp you climb mostly gently on a narrow path through the moorland, with some fine open views over Kenya to the north. As you climb, the trees become sparser and later disappear; even the heathers start to shrink at higher altitudes. However, there is still plenty of interest in the colourful wild flowers.

You'll also see signs of animal life, notably buffalo dung. Shy eland, the largest of the antelopes, also venture high into the Saddle area. Bird life includes the white-necked raven, the tame alpine chat (dusky brown with white sides to its tail) and streaky seed-eater. You'll also see the four-striped grass mouse around your camp here.

Within three hours the path climbs past First Cave: see photograph on p89. After a further 20 minutes of rocky path and tussock grasses you reach Second Cave. You are 800m vertical above Simba Camp, and this makes a good lunch stop. Indeed those with a spare day often camp here, postponing the remaining 450m climb to Third Cave for next day.

Simba Camp

Simba Camp
2650

Second Cave
3450

Third
Cave
3900

Alternatively, the effort of making and breaking camp could be saved by keeping going and spending two nights at Third Cave, with acclimatisation walks on the extra day. (Sleeping in caves is prohibited by the National Park, because fire damage has weakened the rock ceilings.)

The path to Third Cave leaves from behind and above Second Cave. At first it's rocky but not too steep, followed by softer ground, then with large boulders that sometimes block the views of Kibo and Mawenzi. The vegetation thins out markedly, dominated by low heathers, groundsel and Helichrysum. The ground is arid, with river-beds dry for most of the year. It takes only a couple of hours to reach Third Cave from Second. This is the last chance to collect water, so stock up with all you need, and expect to carry some spare water up to Kibo Camp for communal use.

A more interesting choice, if you can spare three days to reach Kibo Camp from Simba, is to follow the indirect route via Mawenzi Tarn: see p92. Since this option affects the whole group, especially the porters, the decision will either have been taken long before you set off or, if the group is small and flexible, should be agreed with the guide on arrival at Simba Camp. After lunch at Second Cave, you would bear left (south-east) to overnight at Kikelewa Caves.

First Cave

Time (average)	**4–5 hours**
Altitude gained	**800m (2625ft)**
Grade	**mostly easy, with some slightly steeper sections**
Terrain	**good path, with no technical difficulties**
Summary	**another day of steady ascent across the increasingly bleak Saddle region**

Make an early start today so that your body has a chance to rest and recover before your midnight departure for the summit. The route makes a steady ascent across the arid montane desert, its greys and browns relieved only by hardy lichens and lonely, brave clumps of Helichrysum clinging to the shelter of big boulders.

Soon after you cross the Northern Circuit path, the path divides. You may continue to Kibo Camp, or bear right up towards School Hut (4730m) – a little-used campsite backed by dramatic cliffs. On this option (decided by or with your guide in advance), the slightly longer ascent today is offset by a slightly shorter summit day. The ascent route to Gillman's Point from School Hut merges with the one from Kibo Hut at about 5100m, just below Hans Meyer Cave: see p85.

Third Cave campsite, with Kibo behind

Third Cave
3900

Kibo
Camp
4700

Going straight on from the path junction, the trail to Kibo Camp leads steadily upward through the rocks and scree, until you sight the large concrete hut, perhaps with tents already pitched nearby. Here for the first time you will meet large numbers of other hikers from the Marangu route, and can compare notes. Marangu hikers will be sleeping dormitory-style in Kibo Hut, rather than camping. (On summit day, everybody descends to Horombo Huts, so the folk you meet here are all on their way up.) The rest of this ascent is exactly as for Marangu: see pp84-5.

Bleak terrain approaching Kibo Camp

Simba Camp to Kibo Camp (indirect)

Day	Start	Finish	Altitude gain m	ft	Time (hrs)
1	**Naremoru Gate**	**Simba Camp**	700	2300	**3-5**
2	**Simba Camp**	**Kikelewa Caves**	950	3120	**6-8**
3	**Kikelewa Caves**	**Mawenzi Tarn Camp**	750	2460	**3-5**
4	**Mawenzi Tarn Camp**	**Kibo Camp**	350	1150	**4-6**

The alternative route follows two sides of a triangle, taking in
Mawenzi Tarn. It diverges from the direct route at Second Cave
(3450m/11,320ft), which is otherwise the Day 2 lunch stop. Instead
of heading south for Third Cave, you bear left to camp at Kikelewa
Caves (3600m). Your third night is spent at Mawenzi Tarn Camp
(4350m/14,270ft), named after the only tarn (lake) on the mountain.
This unique campsite lies under the jagged features of Mawenzi,
with fine views of its northern amphitheatre. This option offers a
better altitude profile than the direct route. The modest altitude
gain on Day 4 is helpful immediately before your summit attempt.

Jagged peaks of Mawenzi

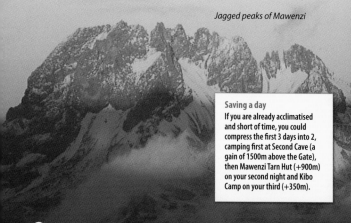

Saving a day
If you are already acclimatised
and short of time, you could
compress the first 3 days into 2,
camping first at Second Cave (a
gain of 1500m above the Gate),
then Mawenzi Tarn Hut (+900m)
on your second night and Kibo
Camp on your third (+350m).

4 The descent (all routes)

You face a protracted steep descent immediately after a sleepless night of unprecedented exertion at altitude. Coming down sounds simple, and most people underestimate it; indeed, many guidebooks barely mention it. However, your chances of falling are always greater on the way down a mountain, and on steep scree they are higher than usual.

There are two main desecent options: Mweka (if you went up by Machame/Lemosho) or Marangu (for Marangu/Rongai). On Mweka, most groups descend to Mweka Camp, a drop of 2795m/9170ft. A shorter option is to overnight at High (Millennium) Camp at 3800m, a descent of 'only' 2095m/6875ft. Inevitably the price is a longer final day: check with your guide and itinerary. On Marangu, there's no choice: from Gillman's Point you descend to Horombo via Kibo Camp, a drop of 2195m/7200ft from Uhuru.

Descending from Stella Point in deep snow

4 The descent (all routes)

For Mweka, you return via Barafu, where you may have a rest after the steep descent from Stella Point over scree and perhaps snow: see p93. You will see people half-running, half-skidding down the scree: with two poles and a good sense of balance you may find this much faster than walking. If you fall, try to relax on the way down and watch out for rocks.

The dust may affect your eyes, nose and throat. Protect your face (with a bandanna or silk balaclava) and don't follow another walker too closely. Before you start, make sure your boots are tightly laced so your toes don't hit against the end. This can cause lasting numbness and later loss of a toenail or two.

Once safely down, you will find beer on sale in camp. By all means enjoy one or two, but be aware that you are still at high altitude and alcohol will have about double its normal effect. It is also a diuretic, and may reduce your chances of an unbroken night's sleep.

Scree-running kicks up the dust

The final day on the mountain is not described separately. From Mweka Camp, the descent is much shorter than the previous day – 1500m/4920ft to Mweka Gate – completed easily by lunchtime. (From High Camp, you have 2200m/7220ft still to lose.) On Marangu, the descent reverses the first two days' climb (1800m/5900ft from Horombo to Marangu Gate), with a lunch stop probably at Mandara Huts. In either case, the trail is steep in places and often muddy: you may be glad of gaiters and poles.

Your last day is precious; with the pressure off, it may seem a shame to hurry it. However, remember that your guides and porters will be keen to return to their families. Some may leave as soon as their work is finished, so expect to say your goodbyes at the final camp, not the Park Gate. This is the time to hand over their hard-earned tips, and if you're lucky, they may sing for you: see p96 for the traditional song. Your group may also wish to organise a speech, song or ceremony: the occasion can make a lasting memory of an unforgettable week.

Porters' farewell, in dance and song

Swahili is the main trading language of East Africa, spoken (as a first or second language) by some 30 to 90 million people. Standard Swahili is based on a dialect from Zanzibar which spread inland during the 19th century. Its use was continued by the European colonial governments that occupied East Africa toward the end of the century. It has adapted and adopted an unusual number of words from other languages, especially Arabic. Swahili is usually written in the roman alphabet nowadays, although 18th century Swahili literature was written in Arabic script.

Kilimanjaro song

Kilimanjaro (x3)
– mlima mrefu sana,
  Kilimanjaro – is a very high mountain,

Na Mawenzi (x3)
– ni mlima mrefu.
  and Mawenzi – is also a high mountain.

Ewe nyokaa (x3)
mbona wanizunguka
  You snake (zig-zag), why do you surround me?

Wanizunguka (x3)
– wataka kunila nyama?
  You surround me, – do you want to eat me as meat?

English	Swahili
hello	jambo
goodbye	kwaheri
please	tafadhali
thank you (very much)	asante (sana)
welcome (you are)	karibu
no problem	hakuna matata
letís go (now)	twende (sasa)
yes	ndiyo
no	hapana
slowly, gently	pole, pole
quickly	haraka
danger	hatari
freedom	uhuru
journey	safari
help	usaidizi
how are you?	habari?
I'm fine/(very) good	nzuri (sana)
I feel (much) better	afadhali (sana)
I am tired	nimechoka
I love you	nina kupenda
I need help	nipe msaada
We love you	tuna kupenda
my head aches	kichwa kinauma
bad	mbaya
hungry	njaa
thirsty	kiu
how much/many?	ngapi?
expensive	ghali
cheap	rahisi
toilet	choo
water (drinking)	maji (ya kunywa)
tea	chai
coffee	kahwa
beer	pombe
ice, hail	barafu
storm	kipunga
elephant	tembo
giraffe	twiga
lion	simba

Sources and credits

Books and maps

Bezruchka, Stephen (2nd ed, 2005) *Altitude Illness: Prevention and Treatment* Mountaineers Books

Pocket-sized summary of the causes, symptoms and signs, with decision trees, tables and case studies, 156 pp, 978-0898866-85-8

Megarry, J (3rd ed, 2005) *Explore Mount Kilimanjaro* Rucksack Readers

The present book contains rewritten, updated and extended material from my larger format book which covered Machame, Marangu and Rongai routes 64pp 978-1-898481-23-2

Moushabeck, M and Schulz, H (2009) *Kilimanjaro: A photographic journey to the roof of Africa* Interlink Publishing

A portrait of the beauty and rhythm of the mountain presented in words and pictures by partners who summited via the Lemosho route; an ideal gift for aspirant climbers, 160 pp 978-1566567534

A general guidebook on Tanzania (and perhaps a Swahili phrasebook) would also be useful, e.g. the latest from Lonely Planet.

Maps

There are many topographic maps, mostly difficult to source ahead of your trip; to buy direct, visit **www.rucsacs.com/kilimanjaro**

Kilimanjaro National Park (2008) map showing the mountain at 1:100,000 (Kibo inset at 1:50,000); obverse carries town plans of Arusha and Moshi; Harms-IC-Verlag 978-3-927468-29-0

Kilimanjaro: Kibo (2008) main mapping at 1:80,000, with town plans of Arusha and Moshi and GPS data; 978-3-9523294-1-2 **www.climbing-map.com**

In Tanzania, the most widely available (and cheapest) is Tombazzi's hand-drawn map of Kilimanjaro National Park (1:83,000 plus summit area at 1:20,000). His map of Arusha National Park is useful for climbing Mount Meru, and both are updated from time to time.

Google Earth

The new high-resolution satellite images on Google Earth are, literally, a revelation. If you haven't got access to this wonderful program, arrange to visit a computer that has. Simply enter *Kilimanjaro* in the 'Fly to' window, then zoom, pan and tilt to explore the mountain and your chosen route. You'll also find links to photos and videos. These links are regularly maintained. The independent website **www.7summits.com** arranged two of my research trips through its agent Zara Travel, Moshi. They offer land-only trips to suit travellers from any country who book their own flights.

Websites

Visit **www.rucsacs.com/books/kilimanjaro** and choose *Links* for selected websites including diaries, blogs and photo galleries; tour operators and background on Tanzania; porter protection, full moon dates and visas. These links are regularly maintained.

The independent website **www.7summits.com** arranged two of my research trips through its agent Zara Travel, Moshi. They offer land-only trips to suit travellers from any country who book their own flights.

Visas

Most visitors need a visa for admission to Tanzania. Britons can use the link from our website; Americans should apply to the Tanzanian Embassy in Washington; others should seek advice from their tour operator.

Acknowledgements

I want to thank warmly all the guides and porters without whom none of my four ascents to the summit would have been so enjoyable – nor perhaps even possible: *asante sana*.

Photo credits

Michelle Cook p80; Travers Cox p44; Jason Kalbfleish p8, p83; Duncan MacDonald p20; Kristin Reynolds p??; Craig Smith p84; www.cellsalive.com p21; Brian Spence p24; all other photographs, including cover, are by Jacquetta Megarry.